ED NOLT'S NEW HOLLAND BALER:

"Everything Just Went Right."

BY ALLAN W. SHIRK

Ed Nolt's New Holland Baler:
"Everything Just Went Right."

by Allan W. Shirk

Copyright © 2015

All rights reserved.

Library of Congress Number: 2015915144
International Standard Book Number: 978-1-60126-464-0

Printed 2015 by
Masthof Press
219 Mill Road
Morgantown, PA 19543-9516

Table of Contents

Foreword v
Acknowledgements vii
Introduction ix

CHAPTER 1: The Formative Years 1
    Baler Problems 6
    Ed Makes a Radical Decision 9
    Let It Snow, Let It Snow! 11
    Blacksmith Engineering 15

CHAPTER 2: Working on the Nolt Special 17
    "Ich Hab's!" (I have it!) 17
    Ed's Baler Emerges: The Nolt Special 21
    Local Investors 23

CHAPTER 3: Moving Beyond Farmersville 26
    A Super Salesman 32
    The New Holland Men 36
    The Original New Holland Machine Company 38
    A Hospital Visit 39
    Ed Moves to New Holland 40

CHAPTER 4: The New Holland Bonanza 48
    Pearl Harbor 50
    Ed and the Baler Boys 52
    Ed Nolt's Roots 53
    A Unique Friendship 56
    Baler Improvements 59
    Ed's Room 62
    Merger with the Sperry Corporation 65

CHAPTER 5: "It Changed Everything" 69
    George C. Delp: Confidant 71
    An Embarrassment of Riches—Too Much of a Good Thing? 74
    The CRELS Foundation 76

CHAPTER 6: The Later Years..85
    Gone Fishing!..85
    Lawn Sprinklers..92
    Visiting the Nolt Home..93
    Family Reflections 94
    In Tribute 98
    Summation...99
APPENDIX: 1964 INTERVIEW 104
ENDNOTES...108
WORKS CITED 114
    Interviews by Author...116
OTHER STORIES 117
    Helping a Farmer 117
    Frugality..117
    Humor 118
    A Wild Ride 118
    A Missed Opportunity?..118
    Sunday Cigars 119
    Air Conditioning...119
    Don't Count Your Chickens…..119
    Strong Hands 120
    Not a Union Man...120
    Seeking Advice 120
    Two Brothers: A Contrast of Personalities 121
    Boys Will Be Boys 122
    Joe Becomes a Believer..122
    Car Shopping 123
    Furniture Shopping 123
    An Unusual Bale Tale 124
    No Picnic 124
    A Dusty Hat..124
    A Reel Story 125
INDEX 126
THE AUTHOR 130

Foreword

This story begins during renovations of the Kauffman Hardware Building in New Holland. The second floor of the building was being re-purposed as the location for a newly planned New Holland Area Historical Society Museum. Author Allan Shirk was volunteering as a painter and while discussing the role the Museum might play in the community, Allan told me of an interview he did with Ed Nolt for a senior class project at Eastern Mennonite College. Since interviews with Ed were a rare occurrence he offered the thought that a copy of that interview might be an artifact that should reside in the new Museum. Allan also related a latent desire of his which was to write a "sequel" to the 1964 interview.

Fast forward a year-and-a-half to the opening of West Hall of the Museum and the placing of the New Holland Machine Company exhibit. Numerous visitors to the Machine Company exhibit would offer interesting and insightful "stories" about Ed Nolt and his baler.

It seemed that although Ed preferred a low profile and disliked attention being called to himself, he nevertheless left an impression on many of his fellow workers and associates. These impressions and therefore the stories, often centered around his occupational prowess, his physical strength, his private and quiet demeanor and his struggle with the overwhelming nature of success that came his way. The thought occurred, "We are a Historical Society that prizes the recording of history. What a shame it would be to lose the memories these stories are carrying!" Additionally, the realization was setting in among family and friends that following generations were about to be deprived of ever knowing about Ed's life and accomplishments.

Several conversations linking Allan's desire to write a follow-up to his 1964 essay and our desire to record these stories took place and the rest "is history." Meetings were held with family, with retired employees of New Holland Machine and input was solicited from anyone who recalled or were told of memories of Ed. Slowly over the months a portrait began to emerge of a person who desired to remain a simple farm boy from Fairmount and Farmersville. Though in the midst of that simplicity, there dwelled a more complex personality that was likely the result of the collision of a humble upbringing with the trappings of success his endeavors led to.

The goal of the following work is to honor this simplicity while also recording Ed's accomplishments, not the least of which was to put the town of New Holland on the world map. This book then, is first for Ed's family near and far as a remembrance of their forebearer. Finally, it is an inspiration to all who have been blessed to reap the rewards of the fruits of his hard labor, his ample hands, his determination and his God-given, keen mind.

-Don Horning
New Holland Area Historical Society

Acknowledgements

I want to acknowledge and thank the many people who assisted me in this undertaking.

A special thanks to Donald Horning of the New Holland Area Historical Society who has been the guiding spirit behind this project supplying much enthusiasm, contacts with people, their stories, photos and documents.

Thanks to Shaun Seymour who described himself as a friend of Ed Nolt. As an engineer at New Holland, he got to know Ed well. He shared a great deal of his knowledge in the form of stories and the perspectives of an engineer.

Thanks to Kenneth N. Burkholder who shared stories, insights, letters from George Delp, and his encouragement to go forward with this project.

Thanks to Frank N. Weaver who generously shared his mechanical knowledge, memories and stories of Ed Nolt. He has given valued support and counsel along the way.

Thanks to Luke Weaver who lives on the Nolt home farm where Ed grew up in Farmersville. He has a deep appreciation for local history and shared stories from the *Ephrata Review*. He was helpful in understanding the Farmersville area as it related to the location of Ed Nolt's garage and barn shop.

Thanks to the Muddy Creek Farm Library and Amos B. Hoover who had helpful insights regarding the Old Order Mennonite ways, stories, pictures, and encouragement.

Thanks to Raymond Zimmerman and The Swiss Pioneer

Perservation Associates for sharing stories and the recorded interview of Ed Nolt.

Thanks to Merle and Phyllis Pellman Good who listened, shared advice and encouragement.

Thanks to the Nolt family for sharing stories during our meeting at the New Holland Museum and breakfast at Yoder's Restaurant. A special thanks to Leon Ray Burkholder and Julia Burkholder for additional information about their grandfather.

Thanks to Marlene Hurst who supported the preservation of Ed Nolt's story and organized the initial family meeting at the Museum to tell stories about him.

Thanks to Rough and Tumble Association in Kinzers that made a special effort to show us an Automaton baler as advertised by the Arthur Young Company in the late 1930's, and permitted us to photograph the Automaton.

Thanks to Brian Frankhouser, historian of the New Holland Area Historical Society, who provided helpful information about New Holland in the 1940's.

Thank you to my wife, Ruth Ann Shirk, who listened patiently many times to the Ed Nolt stories I heard as I was writing and gave me support just by being there for me.

The following people shared valuable contributions through their stories and memories of Ed Nolt: Julia Burkholder, Kenneth Burkholder, Leon Ray Burkholder, David Gehman, Amos B. Hoover, Mabel Nolt Hurst, Henry Martin, Shaun Seymour, Frank N. Weaver, Luke Weaver, and Raymond Zimmerman.

Introduction

I met Ed Nolt through an interesting set of circumstances. In 1964, I was a college student writing a paper for my history seminar. I chose to write about the New Holland Machine Company. I wanted to include the Nolt story in my narrative and requested an interview. Ed agreed with one condition: Only my professor could read the finished paper. I agreed to honor this stipulation and was graciously invited to meet with Ed in his New Holland home. Henry Fisher, whose financial acumen played a major role in the rejuvenation of the New Holland company, also consented to an interview. Later he requested that his comments also be kept from the public record.

My New Holland history paper became a distant memory, until a few years ago. When Don Horning learned that I was perhaps the first person to interview Ed Nolt about his baler, he became interested in my long forgotten paper.

The foremost question in my mind was my promise to Ed Nolt. Was I still bound to that agreement? We began to consider this question with sensitivity to Ed's wishes and his family. But much time had passed since that promise, and there was a growing belief that his legacy should be preserved. How do we honor a man who didn't want to be in the spotlight but whose work was a major benefit to his community and far beyond? While this account is an attempt to pass on that remarkable story, we know Ed Nolt would be quick to give recognition to others who helped make this feat possible. As Ed said, "Everything just went right," but others played a significant part in that reality.

This story begins with a young Mennonite farm boy who doesn't enjoy school, but he doesn't enjoy farming either. How will he find his way in an era when most of his peers spend their entire lives on the farm? More than school, the farm provided Ed with alternatives. As a boy, Ed began tinkering with farm machinery, and, as a teenager, fixed his father's threshing machinery. His father built a little shop on the farm where Ed could fix things.

Although Ed's father, Edwin H. Nolt, was a farmer, he wasn't content to put all his energy into farming; he had many irons in the fire. Ed soon reflected his father's openness to try new things. When only 19, he took over his father's custom threshing business. He also opened a service station in Farmersville. His mother, Mary Burkholder Nolt, also reflects some enterprising thinking. In her role as the Farmersville area correspondent for the *Ephrata Review,* she didn't conform to the usual expectations for an Old Order Mennonite woman of that era. How did his parents influence Ed's life?

Ed was soon trying new technology to improve his threshing operation. He was one of the first in the area to use a combine in place of the threshing machine. New ways bring new demands. Now he needed to bale customers' straw as it lay in the field, but here new technology failed him. The Innes baler he bought didn't work. Necessity dictated—he would try to do something major implement companies weren't able to do—make a baler that worked. It would be a baler one man could operate in the field. One that stopped the plunger's action just long enough to tie bales automatically as the baler moved along. How could he possibly succeed?

CHAPTER 1 *The Formative Years*

Ed Nolt closed and locked the doors to his barn. This would be his shop during the winter of 1936 for a demanding quest. The laughter of the garage boys still lingered in his mind. Their skepticism grew with each of his failures to modify the Innes baler he bought for his custom threshing business. He didn't want any distractions, interruptions, the prying eyes of onlookers, or unsympathetic comments as he had experienced at the garage. His vow to make a baler that worked was more than a matter of ego. He needed a baler capable of handling the straw his combine left scattered behind in customers' fields.

His garage business in Farmersville was doing well but the threshing operation needed a quick fix for the straw problem. Surveying his shop's meager amount of machinery, Ed also thought about his limited finances—he had just purchased his farm a year ago. Could he actually pull this off?

Beyond his eighth-grade education, he didn't have any formal training. Such thoughts were brief and fleeting, replaced by so much more that was going on in his mind. He was accustomed to working with his hands, letting them give shape to what was in his mind. There were no plans laid out on paper. It's unlikely he had a great vision for the future of what would transpire beyond his barn in Farmersville, but he would begin.

Many years later, at the end of his career, looking back on his life's work, Ed Nolt shared others' amazement about how it had all come about. As he said, "Everything just went right" in his quest to build a better baler, but this venture had many more critical junctures than his reflections suggest.[1] From this inauspicious beginning in his small farm shop, Ed Nolt's baler would eventually become a major product of the newly reorganized New Holland Machine Company. It would put New Holland on the map, ultimately becoming an international success. This is the story of a remarkable man whose inventive mind achieved what others had failed to do. His machine would be a one-man operation with the ability to bale and tie material, such as hay and straw, in well-formed bales automatically.

As a young boy, Ed's mechanical abilities were already becoming apparent. One spring morning when the students arrived at school they noticed the teacher's car wasn't parked in its usual spot next to the school building. It was stopped just inside the schoolyard fence.

At noon the teacher walked down to the car and prepared to start it. In those days this required setting the spark advance and choke. Then the teacher gave the hand crank a few quick turns but the car didn't start. One of the older schoolboys looking on stood next to Ed. Little Eddie, as he was known then, suggested to the older boy that he could possibly fix the car if he had a pliers. When the teacher heard this, she got a pliers out of a box in the trunk. Handing it to Eddie, she encouraged him to see what he could do so long as he didn't break anything.

Little Eddie had watched mechanics work on cars. He learned by watching and asking questions. He decided to test what he had learned. Using the pliers, he removed the small drain plug at the bottom of the carburetor. No gas ran out. Then he tapped the side of the carburetor and suddenly gas began running from it. He quickly replaced the plug. The carburetor float had been stuck. Eddie handed

Edwin B. Nolt birthplace on Fairmount Road. Nolt family photo.

the pliers back to the teacher. With a few swift turns of the crank, the car started quickly![2]

Perhaps little Eddie didn't get an "A" in spelling that day, but if auto mechanics had been part of the curriculum, the teacher surely would have awarded Eddie his "A!" This experience foreshadowed where Ed Nolt would excel in the future as he developed his innate abilities. It would not be due to his formal education.

Edwin B. Nolt was born in 1910 on Fairmount Road near Farmersville. His parents were Edwin H. Nolt and Mary Burkholder Nolt. He grew up in the rural Fairmonut-Farmersville community of Lancaster County, Pennsylvania.

In his early years on the farm, it became apparent to his mother that he was special, but in a way that troubled her. He didn't appear to take to farming naturally as was assumed in that era. His mother wondered "what would ever become of that boy." Ed said later, he was never interested in farming and preferred tinkering with machinery in his shop. "I was always fiddling with something," he said. Although he attended school for 8 years, Ed missed many school days due to his lack of interest, and the opportunity to work with his father.[3]

Even though he wasn't a discipline problem, it was apparent to his teachers that his heart just wasn't in his schoolwork. In contrast, his brother Joe was a quick learner who still had time to become involved in schoolboys' mischief. Others remembered Ed as a slow learner who struggled with his studies. Years later many still had this perception of Ed, and some were surprised at his success in life.

Perhaps today educators would have assessed a learning disability as part of Ed's problem. Educators also recognize that not all students' abilities fit into the narrow confines of the traditional "3 R's." He was a good example of students with hands-on skills who find it difficult to have those abilities channeled into book learning.

A family member remarked that when Ed left school, "the teachers were pretty happy to see him go!" So at age 15, his schooldays were behind him. He would find his niche outside the schoolroom walls. Now he could work full time in his father's custom threshing, sawmill and other businesses. He became an important asset to his father's custom threshing business.[4]

Ed discovered his attraction to mechanical things and preferred this work to farming. Machinery was a natural part of life on the family farm. A farmer's ability to make repairs was a necessity. When their machinery broke down, young Ed not only fixed it, he made significant improvements. With his efforts, his father's threshing machine ran better and had fewer breakdowns.[5]

Realizing his son's abilities, Ed's father built a small shed on the farm for such work. It saved him the time and money spent taking his repair work to Art Young's shop at Kinzers during the winter months. While the shop was a practical benefit, perhaps Ed's father also hoped it would be a way to keep him involved with some aspect of farming. Ed's lack of enthusiasm for farming was evident from a young age, as was his inclination to tinker with mechanical things. Could that enthusiasm be satisfied on the farm?[6]

While Ed's father was a man of many enterprises, he was primarily a farmer. For many conservative Mennonites of that era, farming was the bedrock of their identity. It symbolized the essence, the frame of reference, of that identity, heritage, and faith they hoped to pass on to the next generation. There was also a concern that one leaving the farm might also abandon these values and the lifestyle it represented. What would Ed's story be? Would he find a way to use his God-given creativity within the boundaries of his faith and culture, or would he find it necessary to step beyond it?

Ed took over the threshing business from his father in 1929. He was only 19. He proved to be a resourceful young man solving problems to keep his threshing rig running. On one occasion his threshing machine was set up in a farmer's barn. Connected to the Rumely tractor outside, a long belt supplied the threshing machine's power. At some point during the day's operations, the tractor's brake came loose and it began to roll down the barn hill, pulling the threshing machine with it. Alerted to the danger, Ed ran for the Rumley as the belt unhooked. He stopped the tractor before it did any harm to a nearby chicken house. Fortunately the threshing machine hit an obstruction in the barn and stopped there, but this was a serious problem for Ed's operation.

Thought to be site of young Ed's first shop built on his father's farm for him to fix their machinery.

By the next morning when the crew arrived, the problem was already fixed. Ed's solution was a deep, negative-five degree notch in the tractor's brake mechanism to counter the machinery's harmonic vibrations that had loosened the brake. From now on the threshing machine would stay put! The story illustrates what became a life-long pattern of problem-solving for Ed. In his later work on his first balers, he would study a problem, mulling it over until he had a solution.[7]

Ed's business survived the worst years of the Great Depression, and the future began to look brighter. After seven years of operating the threshing business, Ed looked for new technology to improve his operation. In 1936, he replaced his threshing machine with an Allis Chalmers combine. He was one of the first in the area to have such a combine. The combine harvested grain more efficiently, but presented a new problem. As part of the threshing process, farmers were accustomed to having the straw in their barns. The combine left straw scattered behind in the field. Farmers used the straw as bedding for livestock and a significant component of the manure they used to fertilize their fields.

Ed hoped to solve this problem quickly. He traveled to Iowa to buy an Innes baler, and headed home with high hopes. To his great disappointment, when he tried the Innes, it failed miserably in the field. After a phone call to Mr. Innes, Ed gave up on the Innes and looked for a larger baler. This time he bought a larger Case baler. It was little more than a heavy stationary baler put on wheels with an added pickup. The Case was a heavy, unwieldy machine that also proved impractical. It took several men to operate, and required a hefty, three-plow tractor to pull it. Ed began to wonder if he could make a lighter baler to produce lighter bales less difficult for handling.[8]

BALER PROBLEMS

In addition to his threshing business, Ed opened his Farmersville garage in 1929. The family had moved from Fairmount Road to Farmersville in 1925. His garage was located just across the road from his parents' farm. Ed set up shop to repair farm machinery and automobiles in the front half of an old tobacco shed. As he fine tuned his mechanical skills, he gained recognition as an excellent mechanic. Regarding the garage business, Ed said, "I grew into it."[9] While his garage business prospered, Ed still needed a dependable baler for his custom threshing business.

Ed married Anna W. Martin in 1931. They moved into a farmhouse just west of his garage and set up housekeeping. It was convenient for Ed to live close to the garage as he started work on his special project.

In the back of his shop, he began to tinker with the failed Innes baler. He hoped to make this lighter baler work. In the past, Ed was successful in making improvements on other farm machinery in the little shed his father built on the farm. For example, while working in his father's threshing business, Ed replaced the wooden bearings on their rig and made other improvements, resulting in significantly fewer breakdowns. He saved his father costly repairs normally done at Arthur Young's shop in Kinzers, Pennsylvania. Just as he had made improvements to his father's threshing machine years before, Ed hoped to make improvements on the Innes.[10]

Ed's garage business benefitted from the publicity of his mother's efforts. His mother, Mary Burkholder Nolt, was the Farmersville correspondent for the *Ephrata Review*. In addition to keeping people informed about the social "doings" in Farmersville, she included family notes, some amounting to free advertising for her sons' business enterprises.

For example, one year an early cold spell caused an anti-freeze run at Ed's garage, depleting his entire stock. Reporting this in the *Review*, Ed's mother advised him to get more "alcohol" ready for future customers. She wrote, "Fill up Edwin, there are some more cold snaps at the door!"

Ed's brother, Joe, also benefitted from such advertising when he purchased a new 1929 Reo Speed Wagon. In the *Review*, his mother announced Joe's availability to put this new truck to good use. She reported Joe was ready and willing to "do your *draying*" (hauling), or delivering tobacco to warehouses or any such needs. Joe could easily satisfy his customers' requirements with the new, greatly prized, Speed Wagon.[11]

In addition to their mechanical needs, many gravitated to Ed's garage for social reasons. It was a natural meeting place at the end of a day's work for local talk around the stove and games of checkers. Mary Nolt reported in the *Ephrata Review* that "a checker craze has hit our village and some hot games are indulged in." More than a local fad, checker players were scattered throughout the county. Harvey Weaver, uncle to Frank N. Weaver and rural checker champion, ventured into Lancaster to play the city champ. The match ended in a draw, giving the local boys something to talk about for weeks afterwards at Ed's garage.[12]

It's likely that happy-go-lucky Joe was in the thick of these checkers matches. Tall Joe, known as "*Drei Stoechig* Joe" (three-story Joe) was the extrovert who enjoyed the social action. In contrast, brother Ed could be found on the fringes of such interactions. From what we know of his work ethic and mental tenacity, if he played, he must have been a formidable checker player, prone to a quiet study of the game board and his next move. But while the local boys enjoyed their checker craze at the garage, Ed's baler problems posed a greater distraction. It likely accounted, in part, for his more distant demeanor.

During one evening of checkers, Ed was standing off from the action all by himself seemingly deep in thought. When someone approached, and asked what he was thinking, Ed, far from the checker board crowd, didn't answer. He wasn't being rude. He was likely just doing some mental baler "tinkering" there on the sidelines.[13] The failures of the Innes baler stuck in his craw. What could he do to fix it? His business depended on a solution.

So the tinkering began on the Innes in the back of Ed's garage. Customers stopping for gas frequently found Ed slow to answer his ringing service bell. Deeply involved in his baler work, he reluctantly answered its summons. While at the time, such lack of prompt service might have been bad for business, the baler project out back eventually proved far more profitable than all the gas Ed could pump out front! [14]

ED MAKES A RADICAL DECISION

There were few secrets in such a small, tightly-knit neighborhood as the Farmersville community. Ed Nolt's intentions to fix the Innes baler soon attracted doubtful onlookers at the garage. The "boys," as Ed called these local bystanders and checker players, freely shared their skepticism regarding his ability to make the Innes baler work. They watched each development and failure, having quite a bit of fun at his expense.

Others in the neighborhood were skeptical, but still curious, drawn to the garage by stories of Ed's tinkering. Some became inquisitive enough to peer in the garage windows. Ed put up curtains to discourage the gawking, and later for concerns about security. The boys who congregated inside were bolder with their curiosity and their questions.

As failures mounted, Ed became disillusioned with the whole project and the boys' constant banter. One day, when they asked what he would do next, Ed announced, "Well boys, I have decided to make a baler that really works." "Then the kidding really began," he said, "and the more they talked, the stronger the idea appealed to me." [15]

In 1935, Ed bought the Aaron M. Wanner farm across the road from his garage. It was just east of his parents' farm. During the winter of 1936, Ed moved his baler operation into his barn. He locked himself in his shop with a conglomeration of parts for his baler, a torch, drill press and welder, and began to work in earnest on the Nolt baler. Although the boys' derisive comments were external motivation for Ed, he had an even greater internalized drive to meet this mechanical challenge. His threshing business depended on it, and the task engaged him.

Ed began with limited finances and little understanding of what he would do with his baler, but he was confident farmers would want it if it worked. This confidence was another aspect of his underlying drive to succeed. His baler might become profitable, but he never dreamed of the amount of wealth that eventually came![16]

Ed had only the basic tools for his winter workshop, and he had another need. He needed two costly sprockets. After talking with George Zimmerman, who had a nearby machine shop, he decided to make them himself. With the expensive steel plate he purchased, it was important for him to get his design right the first time. He used a scribe to etch the sprocket pattern onto the steel, then drilled, sawed, and filed the sprocket teeth individually. This was an arduous task, enough for some to throw in the towel, but Ed kept at it. It was a beginning. "I fooled and fooled around until I got what I wanted," he said.[17] When necessary, Ed had to stop his work to clean his files because he couldn't afford to buy new ones. It was an unpleasant task, an added burden and obstacle to the completion of his sprockets.

Ed often worked late into the night. He worked with a small light that didn't attract much attention. He put locks on the barn doors so he could concentrate on his work. Throughout his working life, he preferred to work without onlookers. He didn't want publicity about his work to travel beyond his small town. Increasingly aware of his work's potential, Ed became more careful. If he was successful, he didn't want others taking his ideas.

Joe Nolt's farm was adjacent to Ed's. At the end of his plow furrows close to Ed's barn, Joe stopped and walked over to Ed's shop. He was concerned for his brother who was working so intently through the winter months of 1936. Looking up from his work with only a grunt of recognition for Joe, Ed knew his brother was never at a loss for words. Joe was probably quick to voice his concern for Ed and what he was doing. Joe was described as one who spoke his mind—even when not asked for his opinion! Ed was a "thinker," Joe was a "doer." Someone described the difference between the two brothers this way: Ed had a curious mind and took things apart to see how they worked, Joe ran things until they flew apart! [18]

Seven years older than Ed, Joe likely had a big brother's concern as he watched Ed becoming consumed with his mission. He was only 26. Joe voiced his skepticism and his belief that Ed should give up this *"dumbheit"* (fooling around with something that wouldn't amount to much). His solution was for Ed to get back to farming. [19] This was something Joe understood, but it was far from the mind of an inventor like Ed. Joe's case was not convincing for Ed. He kept at his work.

Joe's skepticism would fade a few years later when Ed baled hay on neighbor Jonathan Gehman's Farmersville farm. Excitedly, Joe had seen the light as he exclaimed, *"da baler schaft!"* (The baler works!) He saw some possibilities for his brother's work.[20]

Ed's barn and its winter shop are gone now. Only a picture of the barn remains. Farmersville resident, Henry Martin, identified a photo of the barn where Ed worked. He remembers finding Ed's locks still on the barn doors when his family purchased the farm—maybe they had been installed to discourage Joe's visits as well as others! A few baler parts remained when the barn was razed.

LET IT SNOW, LET IT SNOW!

During a winter snowstorm in 1936, Ed had more than the baler on his mind as he entered the washhouse, stomping snow off his boots. Even though this room was unheated except on Monday wash days, it felt good to get inside out of the howling blizzard. It was the second day of a storm that promised more and more snow. At the supper table, he told his wife, Annie, that even after the storm blew over, roads could be closed for a week. Four-foot drifts already closed some roads and the wind was still blowing.

The next day Ed returned to his workshop in the barn. He looked at his tractor, a ten-ton 30-60 Rumely, used to power his threshing machine during the past summer harvest season. Surely this machine

THE BIRTH PLACE OF THE NEW HOLLAND BALER...

The Simple Story of a Great Product!

YESTERDAY—Just a combination of . . .
Automobile Parts . . .
Washing Machine Parts . . .
and Tractor Parts . . .
BUT—It baled hay better and cheaper and faster than any machine yet designed!

The barn where Ed worked on his first baler.

could be used to clear the roads! His solution was to build a V-shaped plow for his Rumely tractor. How did Ed come up with such ideas?

When problem-solving, Ed's inventive mind drew upon his farm experience for new applications. As a boy, he was resourceful in the little farm shop his father built for work on their threshing equipment. The following story—though only imaginary—surmises Ed's thinking processes as he approached a problem.

As an adult, Ed enjoyed plowing snow. Might this enjoyment have begun in his boyhood years of Pennsylvania winters. Perhaps he made a snowplow for his homemade toy tractor. Fastening a metal plow blade to his tractor, he headed for the stone walk outside and began to push snow. The accumulating snow soon stopped his progress so he slanted the plow to push snow off to the side, but this pushed the light tractor sideways.

Remembering the V-shaped, horse-drawn potato plow they used to harvest potatoes, Ed made a V-shaped plow to move snow to both sides of the walk. His plowing went much better as he cleared the walk. Young Ed's mother, on her way to feed the chickens, stopped to watch her industrious son operate his contraption. "Eddie, what will you dream up next," she mused. While this story is only conjecture, Ed's experiences on the farm did lead to a significant breakthrough in his baler project later on. In reality, Ed did formulate a plan for his tractor's snow plow. He was determined to tackle the snow-clogged roads.

Looking at his Rumely tractor, Ed visualized a curved blade V-plow he would need to push the snow aside as he plowed his way through the snowdrifts. With two tin cans and a tin shears, he began to fashion a model of the plow he wanted to build. The model completed, Ed fired up his Rumely. Skirting the snow-drifted roads, he drove through the fields to George Zimmerman's machine shop. His mission clearly in mind, he showed Zimmerman his model. He told George he needed a V-plow right away!

Together the two men set to work. They cut apart a big steel tank to use as their curved blades which they welded together. After working for three days, their finished plow stood 6 feet high and 11 feet wide. Now Ed was ready to test his plow on the many roads still clogged shut after the storm. It was a great success! He cleared roads to the nearby towns of Bareville, Ephrata, and Brownstown. He was even able to plow Route 322 from Blue Ball almost the whole way to Ephrata. Ed enjoyed plowing snow. He didn't do it for the pay.[21]

Building a plow and clearing roads was the respite Ed needed from the rigors of filing his baler's sprocket teeth that snowy winter and his larger goal of a working baler. Plowing snow became one of Ed's diversions in life. Years later while living near New Holland, he could be counted on to answer the call to clear drifted roads throughout the community. It was something he enjoyed, his way of playing in the snow as he volunteered his time and equipment.

Some years after George Zimmerman's passing, some of his things were given to Raymond Zimmerman, President of the Swiss Pioneer Preservation Associates. While reading through his grandfather's 1936 account book, Raymond came across Ed Nolt's name and the notation, "welding nights." Curious about this brief entry, Mr. Zimmerman visited Ed Nolt to inquire about the welding charge. Ed responded quickly, "Oh, that was the snowplow!" At the end of their conversation as Raymond closed the account book, Ed said that he could just picture that book as he had seen it so often on George Zimmerman's desk.

Then Ed went on to describe the early testing of his plow. The drifted snow had settled for days, and was difficult to plow. When a resisting snowbank refused to yield, one of the Rumely's power train hubs broke and the tractor was disabled. Ed had to figure a temporary fix to get the big machine back to the shop for more substantial repairs. He went home that night and figured out a fix—he would make two large U-bolts to secure the fractured hub. It worked, and he got his tractor home for the needed repairs. Pausing to reflect on the whole experience, Ed concluded that if he had been "smart," he would have attended to the other hub as well, because it broke the next week.

Raymond was amused to hear this obviously smart man referring to himself this way.[22]

In 1958, a major snowstorm became life threatening to a New Holland woman with medical complications in her pregnancy. Now Ed's play in the snow met a more serious need. The woman's medical emergency was drastic enough to require immediate hospital care if she was to survive. Rescue by helicopter was out of the question due to the storm's intensity. Ed was summoned to intervene. Shaun Seymour coordinated the rendezvous via radio from the New Holland Firehall. Ed set out to plow Route 23 towards Lancaster. His goal was to meet a snowplow and ambulance coming from Lancaster. Ed plowed snow all the way to the Leola War Memorial building. There he met the Lancaster rotary snowplow. The woman was transferred to the hospital ambulance for her trip to Lancaster and the urgently needed care that saved her life.[23]

BLACKSMITH ENGINEERING

To some extent the Farmersville boys' skepticism was justified regarding Ed's monumental task. He never had any formal training as an engineer, but had great inherent abilities. While lack of formal training separated him from the professional engineers, Shaun Saymour noted that his ability to visualize spacial concepts of design was an essential trait of all good engineers. He gained a great deal of experience with his work on farm machinery and garage mechanics. Ed worked without drawings doing most of the planning "in his head." He thought drawings and specifications were too limiting. He would go to work building, testing and making improvements. "Drawings can always be done later," he said.[24]

This trial-and-error method, known as "blacksmith engineering," set him apart from professionally-trained engineers. For example, after visualizing all the aspects of the object to be built, an engineer's first task was to lay out the project on paper. Before computers, engineers depended on their slide rules for computations to help visualize the entire project, and to begin drawing each part on paper. Even trained engineers didn't have equal abilities when it came to drawing. Years later computers would greatly aid them in the process. But Ed had to work out his thoughts as he built what was in his mind. He filed these things away in his head and thoughtfully mulled them over before taking action.

In contrast to the engineers, when Ed's experiments were successful, he had to create the patterns used to produce each part. There weren't any plans on paper for the production of these first balers. In the early stages of baler production at Kinzers, these metal patterns hung on the shop wall in the order needed for baler assembly. Over time some patterns included cryptic notations of minor adjustments made as the patterns were used. This proved to be an impossible process for use in assembly line, mass production. One wonders how frustrating it must have been for Ed to have so many ideas in his head without the ability to put them on paper before building.[25]

CHAPTER 2 *Working on the Nolt Special*

When Ed began building his baler, the problem of the plunger's action overshadowed everything else—it was the elephant in the room. The Innes and all other balers shared this same predicament that nobody could solve. The continuous stroking of the plunger packing hay or straw into the bale chamber had to be stopped. The action interfered with tying bales. Somehow Ed had to stop this action long enough to tie the bale while it was still under compression. It was a difficult task. He worked diligently on the problem through the winter months, but all his efforts failed—he had hit the wall!

"ICH HAB'S!" (I HAVE IT!)

Greatly discouraged, he had thoughts of actually giving up. Leaving his shop and its problems behind, he decided to do some spring plowing. Perhaps Ed was taking brother Joe's advice to get back to farming as an alternative if he didn't succeed. It was a fortunate decision.

As he plowed, he struck a rock and the plow mechanism tripped, unhooking just as it was designed to do in order to save the plowshare. When this happened, the farmer would back up, pull a lever on the plow thereby re-hooking the mechanism, and then was on his way again. As Ed reset his plow, a light came on in his mind. It was an "aha moment" of sudden insight. He would transfer this concept to his baler! While the idea was still only in his mind, the experience gave him a new vision of what needed to be done, and renewed his energy for the task.[1]

Returning from his plowing, he met his mother, Mary, near the house with his exciting news—*"Ich hab's, Ich hab's!"* (I have it!) "I've heard that before!" she replied dubiously. But this time it would prove to be true. He was on his way to finding the elusive solution. This was indeed something to celebrate.[2]

Anna W. Martin married Ed Nolt in 1931. She likely had no idea how the for-better-or-for-worse part of her marriage vows would be tested five years later when her husband began work on his Nolt baler. As Ed's intensity with his project increased, Anna confided to a friend that she hoped he would soon find a solution to his baler problems, and she would celebrate with a Milky Way candy bar "when this is all over." It seemed like a small reward for Anna as she supported her husband in his quest, but a Milky Way candy bar and a relieved husband would suffice![3]

Years later at New Holland, fellow engineer and inventor, Shaun Seymour, shared his own struggle finding a solution to a perplexing problem in his work. Under the increasing pressure of the company-imposed deadline—find a fix or the project dies—Shaun shared this dilemma. Ed said, "Yes well, I've been there," and he might have added, many times. He spoke simply but with the wisdom of one whose struggles as an inventor had taught him the difficulty of giving birth to new ideas.

In a 1964 interview with the author, Ed described an "eccentric cam" as the heart of his invention and first patent. Perhaps this was a simple explanation sparing the average person from the much more complex language of engineers and patent attorneys. His first patent describes the workings of his baler in great detail.

Ed's solution was to inactivate the plunger action for a full stroke so the completed bale, still under compression, could be tied automatically. To do this, Ed's two-piece plunger shaft held one shaft inside the other. Secured together in place by a latch, the two shafts operated as one until the bale was completed. Then, on the backstroke, the plunger was held. With the motion of this stroke, the inner shaft unhooked, permitting the continued longitudinal, reciprocating motion of the extending shaft to the end of its backstroke. On the inward, compression stroke, the telescoping inner shaft retracted into the outer shaft, re-hooking the latch. The cycle was completed and ready to begin another bale. Ed had succeeded in transferring the farmer's plow concept to his baler.[4]

A great amount of hard work still remained to be done to create a machine able to function. It didn't happen overnight, but apparently Ed's mind continued to work at night while he slept. Some nights he didn't sleep well as he grappled with his difficulties. In one of his dreams he was working on the plunger mechanism. The dream was so vivid that the next morning he was surprised not to find the finished product on his workbench as it had been there so clearly in his dream. Ed recalled that for days he didn't have anything else on his mind. He believed that without such effort, little could be accomplished. He said, "You have to give it the whole works." This was the persistence, the obsession, that drove Ed Nolt to succeed![5]

Ed Nolt did not invent the baler as some believed. Actually, stationary balers already included some of the elements that Ed built upon. The "gooseneck" pushed the hay or straw down and the plunger pushed it into a bale chamber. When the bale was completed, the gooseneck pushed a grooved block into position at the end of the compressed bale, enabling workers to tie the bale with wire. The first knotters used on Ed's baler were adapted from binders. Good binder knotters had been around for several decades and would only be replaced later along with other baler improvements.

Before the use of combines, threshers left the straw on a big pile next to a stationary baler. This was a convenient way to process straw. Hay was raked into windrows to be gathered using a hay loader and wagon. When the wagon full of hay reached the barn, a hay hook on a rope suspended from the barn peak lifted large amounts of loose hay up to men waiting above in the hay mow. A horse did the heavy lifting, pulling the rope as it walked away from the barn. As the load reached the top, the men pulled the mechanism along a track into the barn and dumped it. Ed Nolt's baler would change all of this. With his automatic baler, one man could do the work that had taken three or four.[6]

Workers at the Shirktown Frolic demonstrate that many hands are needed to operate stationary baler. Photo by author.

The human knotter of the stationary baler. Photo by the author.

ED'S BALER EMERGES: THE NOLT SPECIAL

The machine emerging from Ed's shop was an interesting creation of cobbled together machinery. It could have been christened the ugly duckling. Dubbed the "Nolt Special," it was testimony to his resolve to get the job done under difficult circumstances.

This unique conglomeration of parts came from a variety of sources in addition to the ones he made. Ed said he became a "junkyard rat" salvaging whatever he could use from Sam Plotnick's local yard. Ed's baler had an Innes bale chamber, Fordson tractor bevel gears, and grain binder knotters. A blower from a blacksmith's forge was used to keep the knotters dust-free. The tires and wooden spoked wheels came from a Willys Knight truck.[7]

Ed used his baler in his custom business during the summer of 1937 but there were significant problems. When baling hay on Aaron Good's farm, uneven feeding caused the hay to wrap and stall the machinery. On one occasion bales emerged in clumps. Ed worked desperately, without success, to make adjustments. There were several

Great-Grandpa Nolt's baler, Oct. 25, 1939, in front of Ed's garage in Farmersville. Nolt family picture.

22 ED NOLT'S NEW HOLLAND BALER

Edwin B. Nolt * First Baler * 1936-1937 * Farmersville

The Nolt Special. Nolt Family photo.

Baler and tractor—note wooden spoked truck wheels. Nolt family photo.

problems still to be overcome. With Good's assistance, they took some bales apart and concluded there had to be a remedy for problems with the pickup. The pickup mechanism had to convey equally distributed material into the bale chamber.[8]

Ed reflected, "Returning to the shop, the boys had more fun adding to my determination."[9] For him, this great disappointment was the lowest point in his undertaking. He had come so far. Success seemed so imminent, but it appeared to be slipping through his fingers.

He turned to Arthur Young's shop for help. At Young's he had become acquainted with William Chester Ruth. He knew him well. Ruth was the only African-American in the Gap area to have his own manufacturing business, the Ruth Ironworks. He repaired farm machinery, and created his own inventions. Most notable was his combination baler feeder system patented in 1924. Ruth sold more than 5,000 of these machines throughout the country.[10]

Ed bought what he described as kicker fingers from Ruth and added them to his baler pickup. The fingers improved the baler's performance. Ed continued working on his own pickup design. He designed his own auger system, and replaced Ruth's fingers on the first production model of the Automaton baler at Kinzers. Ed said he wanted his baler to be his own work. He didn't like having "someone else's pieces" on his machine.[11]

Later, the use of Ruth's kicker fingers on his first baler became the source of a rumor that Ed had copied Ruth's ideas in his work. In his years at Arthur Young's, Ed said that he was careful to keep his work and ideas separate from others to avoid situations such as the Ruth incident. As work progressed at Kinzers, over time Ed and Art's roles became more clearly defined in order to avoid such situations.[12]

LOCAL INVESTORS

Some of the most fascinating questions of Ed's story, still not completely answered are: How much money did he need in this initial phase, and where did it come from? While it isn't clear how much the depression impacted Ed personally, it must have had some effect on him and anyone considering investments. Income from his garage and threshing business must have been the basis of his startup. Did he get any financial support from his parents or brother Joe?

Ed made considerable purchases in the year prior to beginning his winter project in 1936: He purchased two balers—the Innes and Case—and a farm in 1935. In 1936 he began to build his own baler. It's likely he approached his baler undertaking without a great deal of money or a plan to finance it—he would cross that bridge when he came it. Even more intriguing, how did Ed Nolt, this quiet, reserved man, convince others to invest in his work? It wasn't in his nature to make a sales pitch to others, but friends and neighbors did support him. Perhaps his total budget wasn't very large, but the risk seemed great during those lean years.

We don't know with certainty who all the early investors were. Some have been identified with differing degrees of clarity. The larger purpose is to appreciate the pressure Ed Nolt felt, not only to ask others for financial help, but also the pressure to succeed. In his Lancaster County culture, failure to build a better baler was one thing, the inability to pay back loans carried an even greater stigma! At some point, Ed felt borrowing from Farmersville resources had been "tapped out." It's not surprising that Ed's mood was sometimes rather somber. For Ed, the intensity of his work and financial responsibilities could have led to some sleepless nights. There was a lot riding on the outcome.

In his most discouraging times, Ed found friends and neighbors who encouraged him. They believed in him enough to loan him the money he needed to continue. Without their support, Ed's project might have died in his shop.

Ed identified his brother-in-law, Moses Kurtz, married to Ed's sister, Katie, as one of his strongest financial backers and encouragers. He also played a crucial role in the baler's future by urging Ed to patent his invention.[13]

Some believe Henry Hoover, who assisted Ed in having stronger twine designed for the baler, might also have been an investor. John

Martin was confident Ed would succeed. He wanted a new baler as repayment for his loan to Ed. George Zimmerman, owner of Zimmerman Steel, probably didn't have money invested, but made steel parts for Ed in his machine shop. He may have done some of the work for little or no charge as his way of helping Ed. Such local money was crucial to keeping Ed's quest alive in its infancy.[14]

Landis Buchen was a trusted friend and successful businessman in the Farmersville area. He built houses, barns and tobacco sheds. He may have built the brick house the Nolts occupied when they moved to New Holland. While it isn't clear that Buchen was an investor, he did act as a financial advisor and money manager for loans Ed made into the 1950's.[15] According to his son Curvin Buchen, he was among the beneficiaries of loans from Ed. Curvin purchased his first car with money borrowed from Ed Nolt.

From the beginning of his working days, Ed didn't appear to have a burning ambition to become wealthy. He was an enterprising young man willing to embrace new technology as illustrated by his innovations in his threshing business. He was simply looking for ways to earn a living outside the farming tradition that had defined so many previous generations. When the necessity of a functioning baler presented itself as crucial to his threshing business, he began an undertaking that pushed his inborn aptitudes to the max. He would build a baler!

People were talking about Ed Nolt. As a boy, Harold Bare remembered listening to the "hunting cabin talk" of his father, Elvin, and some of Ed's other hunting buddies at their Garden Spot hunting camp in Sullivan County. Charles "Bud" Hoober, a farm implement dealer from Intercourse, Pennsylvania; successful farmer, Lester Weaver, from New Holland; and Earl Hurst, founder of the Oregon Dairy complex, were talking about Ed and his budding invention of an automatic baler. At some point in the exchange, Harold remembers hearing one of the men say, with some wonderment, "I think he is going to go places with that thing!" If he was to "go places," he needed to leave his barn shop for a larger venue.

CHAPTER 3 *Moving Beyond Farmersville*

Arthur Young was among those who encouraged Ed to keep working on the baler. Art had his own machine shop in Kinzers, Pennsylvania, near Gap. The Nolts knew Art and had done business with him for years. Art was impressed by his observation of the baler's early field testing. His encouragement soon became a significant proposal: He urged Ed to move his operation to the Kinzers shop and to begin manufacturing balers there.

He had outgrown the one-man operation in its Farmersville setting. His Farmersville investors had likely taken Ed as far as they could go with their financial support. He needed better, larger facilities and more machinery. Even though he may not have fully realized it at the time, that this move would take his baler project to the next level, Ed accepted the invitation.[1]

Kinzers brought a new dynamic to the project. It was a transition from the farm—to make a baler that worked for Ed's threshing business—to the factory; making balers for the market. It's doubtful that Ed Nolt could have taken his baler to this next level alone. If it hadn't been for Art Young's help, someone else would have had to help Ed get beyond the farm. Mass production and the financial backing for a factory on the farm would have been difficult, and beyond Ed's interests.[2]

Ed's first baler was working when it arrived in Kinzers, but it was a rudimentary machine in need of many refinements before large scale

The "ugly duckling" emerging form Ed's barn would soon find a new home at Art Young's Kinzers Shop. Nolt Family Photo.

It works! Ed's first baler parked in Farmersville. Evidence of his success—a tied bale of straw in the bale chute.

production could begin. Even after making improvements, the baler continued to have a characteristic noisiness in the field, but gradually, it was becoming a better machine.

In 1938 Ed was given free run of Art's shop, equipment and workers. In the first year Art's men worked with Ed's, probably doing more routine tasks. The two men's roles had not been defined at this time. How much the two men collaborated working on the baler isn't clear, but Ed acquired a patent for the basic mechanism arresting the plunger action while bales were tied. There doesn't appear to be any question the patent was Ed's alone.[3]

Ed's brother-in-law, Moses Kurtz, urged him to apply for a patent, and to do it immediately. But Ed was strapped for cash and couldn't foresee taking such a step financially. The application process cost approximately $1200.00. Moses Kurtz said he would pay for this, and if the project failed, Ed didn't owe him anything. If it succeeded, he wanted to be paid double. He was well compensated! Ed applied for a patent in 1938.[4]

Perhaps Young's greatest contribution at this level was helping Ed to begin a system for replication. After you have made one baler, how do you produce more of the same? Art introduced the use of patterns into the process. Patterns for each part hung on the wall in the order needed to make baler parts for assembly. This was a slow process that first year. The shop turned out only five balers in 1938.[5]

In 1938 Ed's prototype, the "Nolt Special," received a new name. Art Young's wife, Luetta, suggested the "Automaton," and the name stuck. This would be the name for the Kinzers era balers of the Arthur S. Young Company. Beginning in 1939, with baler number 6, their silver paint with green trim gave the Automaton baler its distinctive identity.[6]

In 1938 the Young-Nolt team built 5 balers and followed them closely in the field. Ed recalled, "We ran after them all summer in the field," to learn what changes had to be made. At the end of the

```
                    ADDRESS ONLY
              THE COMMISSIONER OF PATENTS
                WASHINGTON, D. C.              181        Serial No.  201,089
            Div. 2
            HWJ/rs                DEPARTMENT OF COMMERCE
                                 UNITED STATES PATENT OFFICE
                                       WASHINGTON           February seventeenth, 1941.
                Edwin B. Nolt

                  Your APPLICATION for a patent for an IMPROVEMENT in
                          MEANS FOR BALING MATERIAL
                  filed April 9, 1938 has been examined and ALLOWED with 13 claims.
                    The final fee, THIRTY DOLLARS ($30), WITH ONE DOLLAR ($1) ADDITIONAL
            FOR EACH CLAIM ALLOWED IN EXCESS OF 20, must be paid not later than 6 MONTHS
            from the date of this present notice of allowance.  If the final fee be not
            paid within that period, the patent will be withheld; SEE REVISED STATUTES,
            SECTION 4885 AS AMENDED BY ACT OF CONGRESS APPROVED AUGUST 9, 1939.

                    The office delivers patents upon the day of their date, on which date
            their term begins to run.  The preparation of the patent for final signing
            and sealing will require about 4 weeks, and such work will not be begun
            until after payment of the necessary final fee.

                    When the final fee is paid, there should also be sent, DISTINCTLY AND
            PLAINLY WRITTEN, the name of the INVENTOR, TITLE OF THE INVENTION, AND
            SERIAL NUMBER AS ABOVE GIVEN, DATE OF ALLOWANCE (which is the date of this
            circular), DATE OF FILING, and, if assigned, the NAMES OF THE ASSIGNEES.

                    If it is desired to have the patent issue to an ASSIGNEE OR ASSIGNEES,
            an assignment containing a REQUEST to that effect, together with the FEE for
            recording the same, must be filed in this office on or before the date of
            payment of the final fee.

                    After issue of the patent, uncertified copies of the drawings and
            specifications may be purchased at the price of TEN CENTS EACH.  The money
            should accompany the order.  Postage stamps will not be received.

                    The final fee will NOT be received from other than the applicant, his
            assignee or attorney, or a party in interest as shown by the records of the
            Patent Office.

                    NOTICE.—WHEN THE NUMBER OF CLAIMS ALLOWED IS IN EXCESS OF 20, NO SUM LESS
                           THAN THIRTY DOLLARS ($30) PLUS ONE DOLLAR ($1) ADDITIONAL FOR EACH
                           CLAIM IN EXCESS OF 20 CAN BE ACCEPTED AS THE FINAL FEE.

                                            Respectfully,
            THIS APPLICATION CANNOT BE RENEWED

                                                              Commissioner of Patents.
                    Charles W. Hull,
                    208 Walnut Street,
                    Harrisburg, Penn.
```

The patent application of 1938. Nolt family collection.

LAW OFFICES
SNYDER, HULL, LEIBY AND METZGER
KLINE BUILDING
208-210 WALNUT STREET
HARRISBURG, PA.

WM. S. SNYDER
GEO. ROSS HULL
ARTHUR H. HULL
SCOTT S. LEIBY
LEON D. METZGER
GEORGE H. HAFER
CHAS. W. HULL
ROY J. KEEFER

November 18, 1941.   CHn

Mr. Edwin B. Nolt,
c/o New Holland Machine Company,
New Holland, Pa.

Dear Mr. Nolt:

Complying with your request by telephone today, the following tabulation shows the amounts which you paid to our firm for services in connection with obtaining for you the issuance of United States Letters Patent No. 2,236,628, April 1, 1941:

January 28, 1937	$ 35.00
February 7, 1938	150.00
April 5, 1938	575.00
April 6, 1939	35.37
January 26, 1940	105.00
January 31, 1940	21.91
September 9, 1940	165.00
September 12, 1940	3.75
February 9, 1941	85.00
February 22, 1941	5.50
Total,	$1181.53

All of the foregoing charges have been paid in full by Mr. Nolt to our firm.

Trusting this is the information you desire, we are

Very truly yours,

SNYDER, HULL, LEIBY AND METZGER,

By *Chas. W. Hull*

The Hull letter listing patent application costs. Nolt family collection.

Top: Side shot of baler showing logo and spoked wheels. Photo courtesy of Rough and Tumble.
Right: This brand logo identifies the Ed Nolt balers built at the Arthur S. Young Co. in Kinzers. Photo courtesy of Rough and Tumble.

day, Ed and others "got their heads together" planning what improvements to make before customers used them the next day.[7]

John Eberly and Howard McGinnis were indispensable members of Ed's team. Working closely with Ed, they solved immediate problems of these first balers in the field and made improvements in design. Some of Young's men might also have been involved in this. Regarding this tweaking process, Ed said, "You have to have patience." It was another example of his persistent pursuit of perfection and the continuing challenges to his innovative mind.[8]

After their first year together, Ed and Art defined their separate roles: Ed would focus on manufacturing balers, and Art would work in materials procurement and marketing. Ed secured a loan and built a separate shop at Young's to facilitate baler assembly and to keep his operation separate.[9]

Their hard work was paying off. "Now we know how to make them work," Ed said, with some satisfaction. Increasing demand supported Ed's sense of accomplishment. With 30 balers produced in 1939, the goal became 90 balers for 1940. While Ed's crew focused on manufacturing balers, selling their inventory was also an important piece of this expanding venture, but sales and management weren't Ed's cup of tea. Others needed to fill this vacuum.[10]

A SUPER SALESMAN

Phil Eyster saw the opportunity for a job selling balers in the waning years of the Great Depression. A resourceful salesman, he convinced Art Young that he could sell balers. This wasn't an easy task. He had to persuade potential customers to buy new, somewhat untested machinery from a small company, and pay cash up front. Working on commission, Eyster began his work selling the Automaton balers.

The original sales literature billed Ed's baler as The Automaton of the Arthur S. Young Company, Incorporated. Eyster gained wide exposure with his Pennsylvania Farm Show display and advertising in the *Farm Journal* magazine. He even produced a movie to convince

Pictures of unfinished balers (engines not yet installed) parked along Route 30 in Kinzers. Due to the purchase of used truck and car running gear, gear boxes, wheels, etc., none of these early balers were exactly alike. Photos courtesy of the Nolt family.

Picture of the building complex in which Ed and Arthur Young collaborated to build the first commercially viable baler.

Existing buildings today in Kinzers where Arthur S. Young's shop was located when Ed Nolt joined him.

Shown is the location of the logo on the Kinzers baler with the twine box in foreground. Photo courtesy of Rough and Tumble.

farmers that the twine Nolt used was superior to the traditional wire used by other machines. Twine was safer, Eyster argued, citing the dangers of cattle-ingested baler wire.[11] His hard work was paying off, Eyster was selling balers!

The Automaton
Self-Tying Pick-Up Baling Press

Offers The Best Known Method Of Handling Your Combined Straw And Hay Crop Direct From The Windrow

FAST　　　　CONVENIENT　　　　ECONOMICAL

ARTHUR S. YOUNG CO., INC.
KINZERS, Lancaster County, PENNA.

Likely some of Phil Eyster's first advertising from Young's. It also included a full page of satisfied customers' endorsements for the Automaton. Nolt family collection.

On the farm, Ed's goal had been to make a reliable baler to use in his threshing business. As he came closer to reaching this goal, his role as innovator and inventor interfaced with larger realities. What would he do with the baler beyond his own use? Moving his operation to Young's shop and going public with baler sales escalated the need for answers regarding the future growth of his enterprise. At Kinzers, Ed recognized he was reaching the limits of his comfort zone, interests and finances. Although Ed didn't know it yet, the actions of other men in the county would soon help him find answers to these questions.

The Automaton bales straw under its own power at a recent Rough and Tumble Threshermen's Reunion Steam Expo event. Photo by author.

THE NEW HOLLAND MEN

The story of the New Holland men, George C. Delp, Irl A. Daffin, and Raymond Buckwalter, began with a secret trip to New Holland one spring night in 1940. They were interested in buying the New Holland Machine Company, a small, run-down shop that had fallen on hard times during the Great Depression. They were ambitious, experienced young men eager to begin a financial endeavor of their own—a risky venture even though the depressions's effects were diminishing by 1940. Their limited finances dictated an enterprise of modest scale. Producing Ed Nolt's baler was not part of the picture as these men began their New Holland undertaking.[12]

Afraid of losing their jobs at Dellinger Manufacturing, the men came to New Holland secretly. In 1933, the Dellinger Manufacturing Company of Lancaster bought the small farm machinery plant in Mountville where these men worked. Henry Fisher hired them as his Mountville team. Together they proved their managerial and sales abilities by more than doubling the Mountville business in two years time, but they weren't satisfied to stay there.[13] They talked of exploring other options. They were risk-takers eager to run their own business. They considered reviving the once prosperous New Holland enterprise. Although Mr. Fisher did not accompany the others to New Holland, he worked with them behind the scenes, and waited eagerly to hear the report of their New Holland reconnaissance.

Henry Fisher's relationship within this group, and later at New Holland, was most unusual. A member and later bishop in the Reformed Mennonite Church, Fisher could not hold stock or an office in the corporation. Church members were not to be in business with non-members. Church teachings regarding pacifism and not taking legal action in disputes also influenced his situation. Following the guidelines of his church, Henry would function in an advisory role to the corporation. He gave important leadership in that role to the young company especially securing much needed finances.[14]

The other members of this quartet brought their own considerable talents to the table. Irl Daffin and Raymond D. Buckwalter had proven themselves to be skilled salesmen at Mountville. George Delp's managerial abilities blossomed there as Henry Fisher's administrative assistant. These men were well equipped to ferry Ed's baler venture through the waters of transition to New Holland, and well beyond anything he or they could have visualized in 1940.

Now he was a long way from his barn in Farmersville! Ed gained recognition for his brilliance as an inventor, but these men were gritty visionaries who wrestled with the realities of getting the reorganized company up and running in a world Ed knew little about, and for which he had even less appetite. It was a fortunate confluence of men and abilities—another example of things working out just right as Ed observed later.

THE ORIGINAL NEW HOLLAND MACHINE COMPANY

In 1895 Abe Zimmerman founded his company now being considered by the New Holland men. He began his business repairing machinery for farmers and millers. As he worked in his shop, Mr. Zimmerman, much like Ed Nolt, became curious about the machinery he was repairing. He made improvements and experimented with his own ideas. His first invention was a feed grinder. Other farm machinery inventions followed.

As Abe began to repair gasoline engines, he developed ideas for his own single-cylinder, hit-or-miss engine. In this era before farm tractors, farmers used these engines to power their machinery. Zimmerman's most significant engine improvement was the tapered water tank used in cooling the engine. In unexpected cold weather, the freezing water in other engines damaged the machine. When ice formed in the tapered water box of the New Holland engine, it was forced upward and didn't do any damage. Farmers didn't have the inconvenience or worry about their New Holland engines in cold weather.

Abe Zimmerman's tapered water box clearly shown in this New Holland engine photo. Photo by author.

Incorporated in 1908, Zimmerman's company continued to grow until the Great Depression years of the 1930's.[15]

Prior to the Depression, however, the machine shop's fortunes were also weakened by an unusual set of circumstances. Abe Zimmerman became a convert of the Russelite sect. The Russelites believed the world would end in 1914. For this reason, he began to divest himself of his earthly wealth and possessions. Abe sold his company stock to many neighborhood farmers and businessmen. Over the years as the business continued to decline, stock values fell drastically until they had little value. The company also had an outstanding bank note to be satisfied.

By the late thirties, the company seemed to be a poor investment. If they wanted to gain controlling interest in the New Holland shop, these men would have to buy up New Holland stock scattered throughout the community. There would be many other challenges in taking over the New Holland shop. These were the stark realities the men uncovered on their intelligence mission to New Holland.[16]

A HOSPITAL VISIT

Phil Eyster was a good salesman for the Kinzers operation. Since he worked on a commission basis, his goal was to sell each baler as it was completed. His sales benefitted the whole Kinzers enterprise because they could not afford to carry a large inventory of unsold stock.

Unfortunately, a serious automobile accident derailed Eyster for a time. Convalescing in the Lancaster General Hospital, he had some unexpected company. Raymond Buckwalter and George Delp, two of the New Holland men, came for a visit. They were already quietly buying up New Holland stocks in the community to gain controlling interest in the company. Raymond Buckwalter had heard about Ed Nolt's baler. He was convinced it might be the product they needed to help launch their reorganized company.

While they were likely concerned about Eyster's health, they had an even more pressing question for him—how many of these Automaton balers do you think we can sell? A true salesman, Eyster must have given them a convincing answer. Soon they were preparing their proposal for Mr. Nolt. In the future, Phil Eyster would be changing employers and selling balers out of New Holland![17]

ED MOVES TO NEW HOLLAND

At Kinzers, baler demand continued to increase straining facilities and resources. The 1940 production goal of 90 balers would push Ed's operation to its limits. It became increasingly difficult to meet the demand for product. At this critical juncture, the men from New Holland met with Ed to explore the future of his baler and their company. They negotiated a proposal for Ed to join them at New Holland. Based on what they saw and heard about the operation at Kinzers, they hoped the baler would make their company profitable. Ed recognized he did not have the entrepreneurial vision or abilities of this group from nearby New Holland.

Perhaps Ed's experience with a painter at Young's was the last straw tipping the balance in his decision to accept New Holland's offer. One day Ed saw the painter sitting in front of an unpainted baler and asked him why it wasn't being painted. The painter complained that he was being paid less than another worker, and wanted the situation rectified before he did any more work. Ed informed him that he didn't have any idea about the financial arrangements Art Young had made regarding wages. He was unable to help. The baler did get painted, and later this worker followed Ed to New Holland. He spent much of his working life there—apparently satisfied with the wage scale at New Holland!

While the painter's wages was a small issue, it illustrates Ed's reluctance to become involved in financial things. It wasn't part of his comfort zone, and the thought of taking on such logistics if he stayed at Kinzers was daunting. If he had an opportunity to get out from under such situations, he decided he would take it.[18]

Did Ed seek others' advice as he contemplated this move? If so, who would they have been? Farmersville resident, Henry Martin described Ed as one who played his cards close to his vest, saying, "He was a man who minds his own business, and others didn't find out his business!" It's doubtful Ed consulted with more than a few persons. Should he stay in Kinzers and grow the business along with Art Young, or move to New Holland, a newly-reorganized company that had yet to prove its worth? Either choice had its pitfalls.

Ed probably shared his thoughts about this momentous decision with his wife, Anna. Daughter Vera remembers hearing her parents talk about Ed's work in the New Holland phase. She remembers her father sometimes talking to Anna about new ideas at New Holland, and his skepticism that they would work. It's likely this pattern of interaction between Ed and Anna began much earlier in their married life, including the decision regarding the New Holland men's proposition.[19]

Ed decided to go with New Holland. Unable to afford a clean buyout, the men negotiated a royalty with Ed as compensation, and he went along with the operation as an employee of New Holland. His association with Arthur Young had been valuable. It enabled Ed to put a creditable baler in the field in 1938—a baler that really worked as Ed had announced in his intentions to the Farmersville boys. But early success had simply raised new challenges for Ed and Young. While Art Young believed they could meet the increased production demands, plant expansion and management, Ed was not convinced or interested in these aspects of the business.[20]

Art Young was gracious, but not happy, to see Ed leave. Ed had benefitted greatly from his time at Kinzers. His time there was an important link between his baler's Farmersville origins and the future explosion of demand that New Holland would have the ability to meet. As part of their separation agreement, Art received a cash settlement, Ed's building, and a special discount dealership arrangement with New Holland making his baler sales more profitable. Ivan Glick described the agreement as one with "no losers."

But a few years later as Ed's success and wealth at New Holland grew, Young had second thoughts about their arrangement.[21]

At the time of their parting, neither man could have imagined the baler's success. Art met with Ed and expressed his dissatisfaction. Although he had no legal obligation to compensate Art due to the contractual agreement with New Holland, Ed gave him a sum of money with no apparent ill will. Looking back on the situation, he pronounced Art "a good fella," someone who had assisted him at an important time in the baler's development, but the New Holland men were better suited to meet the growing demands Art and Ed faced.[22]

While New Holland's financial situation was tentative in the beginning, their vision and determination would take Ed's baler from his Kinzers' shop to the next level: mass production. The economic realities of this merger freed Ed from the financial responsibilities he didn't want or have the desire to perform. He could continue to do what he loved most—tinker in his shop at New Holland where he would carry on with refinements to the baler and development of new models for years to come.

Henry Fisher's talents were well suited for dealing with New Holland's early financial need of capital. When local banks refused loans, Henry journeyed to Philadelphia's big banks for money. During one interview, the banker kept asking to see the company's corporate tax returns. Henry deflected the question as long as he could before he finally produced the meager information from his pocket. After a brief perusal, the banker advised Henry that it would likely be wise if he didn't show this to many people if he wanted to borrow money!

Fortunately, instead of simply denying New Holland a loan, the bank began to educate Mr. Fisher and his small-town firm about finances in the big leagues. New Holland hired Ernst and Ernst to help them draft a financial plan the bank requested. Paul Lyet was quite helpful in this whole operation, and Mr. Fisher hired him away from the Philadelphia firm to become New Holland's accountant. He

AGREEMENT

This agreement made in duplicate this 20th day of August, 1940, by and between Arthur S. Young Co., of Kinzers, Penna., Company hereinafter referred to as Young, and the New Holland Machine Company hereinafter WITNESSETH THAT:

For and in consideration of their mutual grants and undertakings and in further consideration of $10.00 each to the other in hand paid, receipt of which is by each hereby acknowledged, the parties hereto agree, covenant and grant to each other as follows:

1. In consideration of Young relinquishing all rights and claims to the manufacture and distribution of the Automaton Self Tying Pickup Bailing Press designed and presently being manufactured by Edwin B. Nolt, Jr., of Farmersville, Penna., New Holland agrees to pay Young Fifteen Hundred ($1500.00) Dollars Payable upon execution of this contract by note due January 1, 1941.

2. New Holland further agrees to have Edwin B. Nolt, Jr., transfer and set over to Young the plant and grounds at Kinzer, Pa., valued at Ten Thousand Dollars ($10,000.00) in and on which the Automaton Baler is now being manufactured by the aforementioned Nolt. Possession and full rights of occupancy to be given as soon as possible and not later than November 1, 1940 with full deed and title to be conveyed January 1, 1941.

3. Young further agrees to turn over and transfer to New Holland all patterns, dies, jigs, fixtures, customer prospects, correspondence, literature and all other information, etc., pertaining to the manufacture and sale of the Automaton Self Tying Pickup Baling Press.

4. New Holland further agrees to permit Young to distribute these machines and repairs for them to the retail trade only, allowing him a special distributors discount of 25% and an additional 5% for cash.

5. New Holland further agrees to sell twine for these balers to Young at their cost price plus a reasonable handling charge.

6. Young agrees to maintain at all times full list prices as may be designated by New Holland on new balers, baler repairs and twine. If at any time it can be shown that Young does not adhere to or maintain the retail prices set up by New Holland the distributing agreement contained in this agreement may be canceled at the option of New Holland.

7. Young also agrees to refrain from manufacturing or being a party to the manufacture of pickup baling machines of any kind for at least ten years except in a laboring or sales capacity with a manufacture of Pickup Baling Presses already in existence.

The signing of this agreement constitutes a full agreement to, and acceptable without reservation, of all the provisions and terms hereof by the respective signatories.

Executed at Kinzers, Pennsylvania, on the date hereinbefore appearing.

ARTHUR S. YOUNG COMPANY (SEAL)
BY ARTHUR S. YOUNG
PRESIDENT
ATTEST:

H.B. KENEAGY
SECRETARY

NEW HOLLAND MACHINE COMPANY (SEAL)

BY IRL A. DAFFIN
PRESIDENT

ATTEST: G.C. DELP
SECRETARY

THIS IS A COPY OF THE ORIGINAL AGREEMENT BETWEEN ARTHUR S. YOUNG AND NEW HOLLAND.

A copy of the agreement between Arthur Young and New Holland Machine Company signaling the end of baler production at Kinzers and the beginning of production at New Holland Machine. Nolt family collection.

brought valuable financial expertise to this young endeavor. Even so, the bank kept New Holland on a short financial leash in these early years. They had to work hard to keep the cash coming.[23]

Two other men, John Eberly and Howard McGinnis, were assets to New Holland in another way. These men worked closely with Ed at Kinzers and accompanied him to New Holland. With Ed, these men would help engineers at New Holland to incorporate all the baler assembly knowledge they carried with them in their heads! It seemed like a precarious way to transfer such valuable information, but it was the only possible way. Mass production required clear, concise plans. Getting this information on paper became a necessity. The Young-Nolt Automaton baler from Kinzers evolved into the first New Holland Automaton.

As the New Holland operation grew, gifted men without engineering degrees—blacksmith engineers—still emerged from within the company's ranks, but over time professional engineers became dominant. Ed Nolt, Larry Halls, Dick Eby, and A. D. Mast were examples of the blacksmith tradition. Ed Nolt's ideas and persistent work continued at New Holland.

The move to New Holland proved to be a good one for Ed and the company. Ed soon learned of advantages of going with New Holland. The company had the ability, for example, to buy baler parts, such as wheels, for much less than he had paid at Young's. Although their venture began with limited operating capital and much hard work, before long the New Holland men realized they had discovered "a gold mine in their own backyard"—Ed Nolt and his baler! While they would go on to develop other products, the baler was key to the company's early profitability. Without it the company may have struggled along in the small-town mode of its predecessor.[24]

The New Holland group was fortunate that Ed chose to stay with a local company. While there was only mild interest from major implement manufacturers, relocating to another state probably didn't appeal to Ed. Another aspect of this local connection was the special bond Ed shared with George Delp. George spoke Pennsyl-

NEW HOLLAND
"Automaton"
PICK-UP BALING PRESS

The Pick-up Baling Press You've Been Looking For!!!

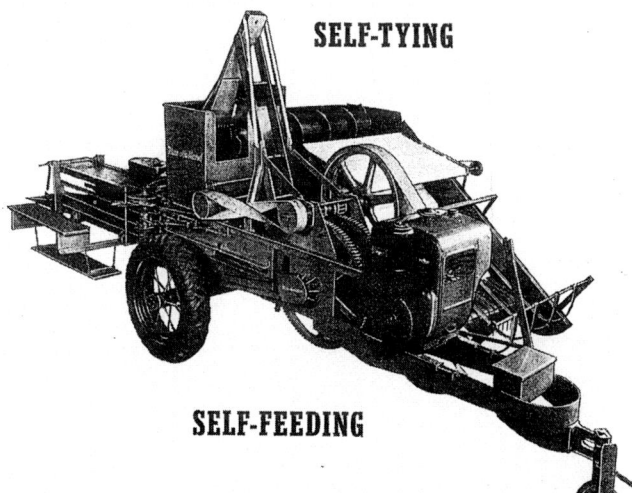

SELF-TYING

SELF-FEEDING

- *No wires to stick or tie--No blocks to drop*
- *Much greater capacities with less labor*

NEW HOLLAND MACHINE COMPANY
NEW HOLLAND - Lancaster County - PENNSYLVANIA

This ad, one of the first from New Holland shows the rapid transition of the Automaton from Kinzers to its new home. There is speculation some of Young's silver and green bailers were covered over with New Holland red in the transition.

The
NEW HOLLAND LINE
Includes

Limestone Pulverizers	V-Belts
Jaw Crushers	V-Belt Drives
Roll Crushers	Feed Mills
Hammer Crushers	Engines
Elevators	Electric Motors
Revolving Screens	Concrete Mixers
Vibrating Screens	(with or without Power Lifts)
Dewaterers	Grey Iron Castings
Belt Conveyors	Semi-Steel Castings
Apron Conveyors	White Iron Castings
Conveyor Belting	Warm Air Furnaces
Baling Presses	Power Lawn Mowers

Belting (Rubber and Canvas)

NEW HOLLAND MACHINE COMPANY
NEW HOLLAND, Lancaster County, PENNSYLVANIA

In addition to the Automaton baler, this ad features the full New Holland line of products offered by the newly-reorganized company in 1940.

vania Dutch, Ed's preferred language. They frequently conferred in Dutch. This was a significant shared cultural connection. Conversing in Dutch was comfortable for Ed and familiar. It was part of his identity and heritage. With this relationship came trust. He wasn't dealing with strangers or a large corporation. These were good men, local men, and they struck a deal that would carry all of them beyond their wildest dreams! Chief Engineer, Larry Skromme, didn't speak Pennsylvania Dutch and didn't always appreciate being odd-man-out in such conversations. He frequently entreated the two men to, "Speak English!" [25]

CHAPTER 4 *The New Holland Bonanza*

When Ed Nolt arrived in 1940, New Holland could be described as a healthy, prospering town, the hub of an agricultural community. *The New Holland Clarion* ads of that day posted a variety of local businesses including the following: car dealerships and auto repair shops, the New Holland Sales Stables, the Ritz Theater, and Rubinson's Department Store. In town one could smell the pleasant aromas from Wright's Bakery. The September 27, 1940, *New Holland Clarion* included the first ad and picture of the "New Holland Pick-up Baling Press" offered by the newly-reorganized New Holland Machine Company. That year the company also began its tradition of giving employees silver dollars at Christmas. In 1946, Clyde Kauffman returned from World War II, and opened his hardware business in the building now occupied by the New Holland Area Historical Society. This was the beginning of a new chapter for the town. In a few years New Holland would provide jobs for many in nearby communities, and connect it to the rest of the world.[1]

Ed Nolt and his baler were still an unknown quantity being introduced into the scene. While the Kinzers years showed promise, it would take some time for this young, Old Order Mennonite "farmer" to find his niche at New Holland.

At times the divide between professional engineers and skilled but untrained "blacksmiths" was apparent. Although encouraged to

The 'New Holland' Pick-up Baling Press

Self Tying — *Self Feeding*

- NO BLOCKS TO DROP
- NO STOPS TO CLEAN FEED HOLE
- LESS LABOR AND GREATER CAPACITIES
- NO WIRE TROUBLES
- USES STRONG CHEMICALLY TREATED TWINE
- LIGHTER BALES, MORE EASILY HANDLED AND OPENED

THE NEW HOLLAND LINE INCLUDES
ENGINES—DIESEL AND GAS   FEED MILLS   WARM AIR FURNACES
BELTING—RUBBER AND CANVAS   CASTINGS—GREY AND WHITE IRON

LIMESTONE PULVERIZERS, JAW CRUSHERS, ROLL CRUSHERS, HAMMER CRUSHERS, ELEVATORS

REVOLVING SCREENS, VIBRATING SCREENS, BELT CONVEYORS, VEE BELT DRIVES, POWER LAWN MOWERS

New Holland Machine Company
New Holland, Lancaster County, Pa.

Taken from the September 27, 1940, New Holland Clarion, *is an early advertisement for the first balers produced by the New Holland Machine Company. This ad appeared exactly five weeks after NHMC's purchase of the rights for the baler!*

consult Ed with their engineering problems, not all professionals were inclined to do so. Early on it became apparent that for the company to mass produce a quality product it would have to move beyond the Kinzers assembly model. Engineers would increasingly influence and control this process. While President Delp and others in the top echelons of the company always treated Ed with respect, some in the lower echelons of engineering were reluctant to cross this divide as the following story illustrates.

In one situation, during baler development, engineers faced a crisis. In their trials, the baler was tearing itself up. The problem was located in the packer tines delivering hay to the bale chamber. To everyone's consternation, the force feeder mechanism continually shattered creating havoc. After listening to the professional "baler boys,"

Ed responded to George's Pennsylvania Dutch, *"Ed, was saughts du?"* (What do you say?) He asked the engineers if they had considered making the part from aluminum.

At that time engineers thought in terms of cast iron or heavy steel for their creations. Some were horrified by the very thought of using aluminum! Notions of using aluminum reverberated through the vested interests of the Belleville plant. Some were concerned about keeping their jobs if aluminum began to replace iron castings. Despite such concerns, when tried, Ed's suggestion of an aluminum part proved to be the needed solution. Ed had learned about the properties of aluminum from engineer Shaun Seymour and others. Aluminum with its lighter weight and reduced mass created a less forceful dynamic in the baler action.

One of the professionals summed up the situation saying it took a farmer with manure on his boots to tell us how to do this! The reality was that without this "farmer," none of them would have been employed at New Holland. The other reality was that these engineers' abilities were essential to the mass production that made New Holland a household brand. Across the divide, each was essential.[2]

PEARL HARBOR

As the New Holland operation began to find its stride, the company made significant internal improvements which included adopting a cost and accounting system. Plant modernization was done on a limited scale. It was important to develop a network of salespersons and dealerships. As the baler's success became more widely known, New Holland was flooded with baler orders. Just as the company appeared to be gaining momentum, its future was seriously threatened, as was the nation, by the Japanese attack on Pearl Harbor. World War II had reached America's shores and the impact would be felt in every segment of life. Many industries shifted to the production of military goods with raw materials prioritized for the war effort.

For New Holland, supplies of steel, engines, tires and many other materials dwindled. The War Production Board made allocation decisions that severely limited New Holland's ability to fill orders. When Irl Daffin wasn't successful making New Holland's appeal to the government, Henry Fisher journeyed to Washington, D.C., himself to plead the company's case. Ed Nolt said, "Henry Fisher was no ordinary man, he could talk a lot of people into doing things they didn't want to do." Fisher said he would be back when he got the answer he wanted, and he got it![3]

Meeting with Agriculture Department officials, Fisher argued the new baler was essential to food production. Using this new, automatic baler required only one person for its operation. If not stated, the implication was that such a labor saving device meant fewer workers were needed on the home front in a time when increasing numbers were being drafted into the armed forces. It was an interesting situation for Henry Fisher, this pacifist, conservative Reformed Mennonite and future bishop, but his success in Washington was vital to New Holland's continuing operation during the war years.

The government granted New Holland status as a class "C industry." The company did not have to switch to manufacturing military goods and could continue producing balers. The "C" classification simply gave New Holland a "hunting license" to procure needed materials, but there was no guarantee of success. Mr. Fisher met Paul Newton, a former War Production Board employee, while in Washington and hired him to manage the newly-acquired Hertzler and Zook company in Belleville, Pennsylvania. Mr. Newton's Washington connections likely helped the company in materials procurement. Although unable to operate at full capacity, New Holland continued baler production during the war years and kept the company going in this difficult time.[4]

Although New Holland was able to continue production during the war years, its operating capital was severely limited by the taxes on its profits. Since the company's earnings were low as a start-up company in 1940, its tax assessment base reflected this situation. Increasing profits after 1940 were deemed excessive, subjecting New Holland to a 90% excessive-profits tax! In 1944, according to *Fortune Magazine*, the company had $5,000,000.00 of sales but only realized a profit of $180,000.00. The company needed to move its inventory quickly and couldn't afford to sell many balers on credit. This was another challenge for the young company to resolve.

During the war, government actions also led to a freeze on wages. Wages were low as New Holland began operations in 1940. During the war, government orders kept wages low and the company was unable to make changes. Low wages created problems for the company that was trying to attract and satisfy new employees. One solution was offering the opportunity to work up to 60 hours a week so that overtime wages helped offset low pay. With the end of World War II, the company's survival mode relaxed and the future brightened.[5]

ED AND THE BALER BOYS

When Ed Nolt cast his lot with the New Holland men, he became a company employee with his own room in the Experimental Division. Here he could continue work on baler refinements. He had access to any shop equipment needed for his work. Engineers were encouraged to consult Ed individually regarding their projects and problems. Such consultations were a fulfilling, life-long role for Ed at New Holland. Sometimes in informal, individual contacts, Ed heard about baler design problems stumping other engineers. He had time to ponder the problem before a general meeting with the "baler boys."

President Delp chaired many of these meetings of a dozen engineers. Addressing the problem before the group, Delp surveyed individual members for their input. Beginning with whomever was sitting next to Ed, Delp went around the circle, saving Ed for the last word. After others had spoken, turning to Ed, George, addressing him in

Pennsylvania Dutch, would say, *"Ed, was saugst du?"* (Ed, what do you say?) "Yes, well…," Ed would begin formulating some kind of "blacksmith fix" he believed would solve the problem.

In one product meeting during a baler's development, the problem was a shear bolt's malfunction. Engineers discussed making the bolt heavier to solve this problem. Finally it was Ed's turn to speak in the circle. He believed the problem was in the flywheel bushing and its edges. He proposed removing the sharp edges to solve the problem. George Delp's, "That's what we'll do," frequently ended such discussions with an endorsement of the blacksmith fix.[6]

In some of these meetings, Ed appeared to be asleep while others were discussing issues. During one Engineering Review meeting in the Sperry era, a new baler model being developed by engineers was under discussion. When George Delp asked the "napping" Ed what he thought about the project, Ed predicted there would be an "awful lot of vibration in that design." When field tested, the new baler was indeed plagued by excessive vibrations.[7]

ED NOLT'S ROOTS

Engineer Shaun Seymour began to visit Ed in his New Holland shop. Ed had an inquisitiveness about Mr. Seymour, this young man who seemed so different from his own provincial Lancaster County background. All his life, Ed referred to himself as a farmer. That identity included his religious heritage and character. His preference for speaking Pennsylvania Dutch conveyed some of those values and orientation.

One can get a better understanding of who Ed Nolt was with more knowledge of his Old Order Mennonite background. The Nolts attended the Old Order Groffdale Mennonite congregation. Historically speaking, in the mid-nineteenth century, the Groffdale Church was located on the fringes of German-speaking territory. This exposed the congregation to more English influences than its Weaverland Church center.

Those who wanted to preserve German regarded language as the most crucial vehicle for transmitting belief and practice from one generation to the next. They saw the English language as inadequate for this task, and some believed the desire to use English was a denial of their roots, a simple matter of pride—"English fosters pride."[8] For many, language was the bedrock of conflict, the flashpoint igniting dissension concerning other modernization issues in the church. The singers' table became a focal point for the conflict over language in congregational life, and a concern of Ed's grandfather, Peter Nolt.

As the ministry waited in an anteroom, the worship service was begun by the laity at the singers' table. Song leaders sitting there announced the congregational hymn. The leader did not stand. That would have been an act of pride. As they decided on the hymn to be sung, sometimes a hymn in English slipped in. This happened most frequently at funerals when the greatest mixture of German and English-speaking people were present. In these situations, English hymns and partial use of English in the service became most prevalent for the benefit of those who didn't understand German. Bishop Jonas Martin struggled to keep Groffdale in line, but the language barrier was eroding due to the bold ways of some Groffdale brethren at the singers' table.

With regards to this conflict, Amos Hoover wrote the following: "The Old Peter Nolt, father of Ed and grandfather to 'Baler Eddie' Nolt, did not allow his descendants to sit at the singers' table. He said that is where all the disputing over language took place..."[9]

Although we don't know how successful grandfather Nolt's family decree was, it's likely that some of his concern about conflict and pride filtered down to his grandson's generation. We can only guess the extent of this influence regarding Ed Nolt's reserved nature and desire to keep a low profile.

In 1893, the Old Order Weaverland Mennonite Conference withdrew from Lancaster Mennonite Conference. Sunday Schools, services in English, and the use of a pulpit were all divisive issues.

Emerging from this division another significant church teaching was that members should live simply without self-promotion. Any behavior that elevated one above other members of the church body, drew attention to oneself, or caused others to notice you, was banned.

Personal photographs were one of the specific ways this was addressed. Members began to destroy their family photos. Posing for a newspaper photo was grounds for a required confession in the church. Some of this emphasis on a quiet, humble lifestyle, and keeping a low profile continues today.[10]

When automobiles first appeared on the scene, an elder church leader predicted there was little need for concern—only the wealthy could afford them. But as cars became affordable for the average American, the issue of car ownership grew. For several years, members owning cars weren't considered to be in harmony with the church and didn't take communion. Families were being excommunicated from the church for owning automobiles. There was a growing fear that this practice would destroy the church. After Bishop Jonas Martin's death in 1925, the dilemma continued to trouble new bishop, Moses Horning. Factions in the church began to drift apart with the ultimate division on May 1, 1927. This was the last time the whole congregation worshipped together. Bishop Moses Horning no longer made cars a test of communion or church membership. The church would accept modern technology and approved the use of automobiles and farm machinery. However, automobiles had to be black, including the chrome bumpers and trim.

Followers of Joseph Wenger opposed owning cars and the use of some modern conveniences. They would use farm machinery without rubber tires, but not cars. They withdrew from the Horning group under Joseph Wenger's leadership to form the Groffdale Old Order Mennonite Conference. To this day, the Horning and Wenger groups still worship at the Groffdale Church on alternating Sundays.

By the 1950's, many Old Order Horning Mennonite congregations still conducted their services in German, had no Sunday Schools or mission outreach, no summer Bible schools or youth activities. Most Horning Mennonites were farmers living in northeastern Lancaster County. This was the religious and cultural context of Ed Nolt's life as he began to learn more about Shaun Seymour. Church members like Ed, had to find their niche within the church, to bend some of the rules without the perception of breaking them.[11]

Not all observers of Lancaster County's "plain people" were sympathetic to what they saw as the peculiarities that divided and defined them. Combined with a "country-bumpkin-farmer" stereotype, it gave those who felt it, or accepted it, considerable emotional freight to carry. Shaun Seymour, who was new to Lancaster County, would make the effort to go beyond the stereotypes.

Shaun Seymour and his wife, Mary, arrived in New Holland to begin his job there with little awareness of the county's religious composition. His curiosity gradually led to involvement with Ed Nolt.

A UNIQUE FRIENDSHIP

A young engineer, Mr. Shaun Seymour, would ultimately reach across the engineer-blacksmith divide, and develop a unique friendship. He was graduating from Cornell University in June, 1956. During his senior year, Shaun's initial job search included New Holland, but when there was no response from that quarter, he made plans to accept a position in California.

A December 1955 phone call from New Holland's Chief Engineer, Mr. Larry Skromme, put Shaun's plans on hold. He agreed to a breakfast interview meeting at the Statler Hotel in Ithaca, New York. During that breakfast conversation with Mr. Skromme, Al Best and George Delp, Shaun expected questions about his grades and resumé, but George Delp wanted to hear about his community involvement as a volunteer. Seymour told them about his volunteer work as an Eagle Scout. Such participation came easily for Shaun. His parents encouraged their children to volunteer, and modeled their commitment through their own service. George Delp shared their belief and promoted it within the company. Seymour had answered well.

During the meeting the men talked briefly about Ed Nolt and the Model 66 baler, their latest product. The previous summer Shaun had operated a Model 66 baler on an Oriskany, New York, farm. He was impressed and described it as "a super baler!" It was one of the things that attracted him to New Holland.

A few weeks later Shaun and his wife, Mary, came to New Holland for a tour of the plant and community. Shaun decided to accept the job and began work in June, 1956. When the Seymours arrived in New Holland on a Sunday afternoon, they didn't know anything about the Amish or Mennonites. They also learned about Pennsylvania's Blue laws. Unlike New York state, stores here were closed on Sundays. The Seymours couldn't find a grocery store to buy the basics needed to begin housekeeping.

A few days after he began work, a secretary told Shaun that President Delp wanted to see him. Apprehensive, he headed for the president's office wondering what he had done already to deserve such a summons. To his relief the topic was volunteering at the New Holland Community Memorial Park. He was "volunteered" to help Bob Ressler with the employees' company picnic, a big event held yearly in the park.

Shaun was in charge of the children's games as one of his volunteer duties. As a result of this involvement, he became a long-time park volunteer and member of the New Holland Community Memorial Park Association. Later he served as a building code official. His community participation was just one example of the many ways New Holland's employees were encouraged to volunteer their talents for the benefit of their communities. Their involvement in municipal governments, charitable organizations, fire companies and other organizations were a tribute to George Delp's promotion of volunteering.

After a year as an intern-trainee of the Engineering Department, Shaun chose to specialize in field testing New Holland equipment. He became involved in work on the Model 166 self-propelled baler. As a junior engineer, Shaun also worked on patent information and avoiding infringement. He designed farm materials handling equipment, such as bale elevators, in the Farmec division. He was not directly involved with Ed's work.

Although he had heard about Ed Nolt, it took some time for their association to develop. As they met, each became curious about the other and their different cultural backgrounds. Ed reminded Shaun of his grandfather, Howard Seymour. He was a watchmaker fitting the blacksmith-engineering tradition. For Shaun, this association influenced his attraction to Ed and their slowly growing friendship.

Ed worked in the Experimental Division. There he had a good team of engineers helping him. Jim McDuffie, Jim Holiday, Otto Luek, and Pete Sturla worked with Ed. After the group's deliberations, Otto Luek put Ed's ideas on paper. It was something Ed couldn't do in the interface with the Engineering Department. His team was essential in the design of hay tools, forage harvesters and other products in addition to balers.

Shaun began a pattern of taking a break from his work in Engineering, and strolling over to see Ed in his room at Experimental. They might talk about challenges faced in their work or just talk. He was willing to learn from Ed and Ed from him. Shaun came to consider Ed his mentor. There was a growing mutual respect. He encouraged other engineers to consult with Ed when they had a problem. As the frequency of these visits increased, Chief Engineer, Larry Skromme, took notice and had a chat with Shaun regarding the amount of time he spent there hanging out.

As Seymour continued his visits with Ed, he became more comfortable answering most of Ed's questions about his ethnic background and life experiences as a native of New England and New York. The troubling question Ed eventually raised had to do with religion. When Ed asked what church he attended, Shaun evaded answering. He feared his answer would jeopardize their growing friendship. The truth was he didn't attend any church. What would Ed think of him if he knew this? So Shaun avoided answering Ed's questions until one day he decided Ed deserved an answer. They were fishing leisurely on the Chesapeake Bay, and the time seemed right.

Shaun's answer wasn't a simple one. His family's religious background had a good bit to do with his answer. It involved his Roman Catholic mother's ignoring the prohibition regarding marriage outside her church. She married an Episcopalian in the early 1930's. Her church didn't approve of their Vermont civil service, or her marriage to a non-Catholic.

Excommunication from the church impacted her and the family in numerous ways. Perhaps most difficult for Shaun was his aunt's funeral years later. He was required to wear a black armband, and wasn't permitted to be a pallbearer for his favorite aunt. The armband signified his lack of good standing in the Catholic Church. Later, his mother was denied burial in the church cemetery. Shaun hadn't shared this painful story with many. Other than his wife, Mary, Ed was likely the only person in New Holland to know.

How would Ed respond to such a story? Considering the boundaries of his own faith, his answer was somewhat surprising. After hearing Shaun's story, a man of few words, Ed's response was, "That's not God's will!" It succinctly summed up his feelings. The divide here wasn't engineering degrees, it was church history. Religious persecution in Europe that brought Ed's Mennonite ancestors to the New World likely resonated with him as he heard Shaun's story. He recognized others, like Shaun, also had been wounded in the name of religion. He was able to reach across this divide to accept Shaun just as Shaun had disregarded the professional divide other engineers felt. Their friendship not only survived this revelation, it deepened.[12]

BALER IMPROVEMENTS

The Nolt Special baler that emerged from Ed's Farmersville shop became a distant relic in comparison to the progressive refinements of succeeding models. In 1940, Model 73, billed as the New Holland Automaton, became the first baler produced after the move from Kinzers to New Holland. During the war years, improvements on Models 75 and 76 continued. By the end of World War II, Model 76 was a very reliable baler.

While New Holland's balers were very efficient at baling straw, hay presented other problems. The baler's pickup, located on the left side, was fine for straw; it was less efficient picking up hay. The left side arrangement didn't work as well for hay because baling worked best if the hay was picked up stem first. When picked up head first, some of the crop was lost. This problem led to a radical design change.

Switching the pickup to the right side on the Model 77 solved the problem. Another upgrade, a new pickup system eliminated the canvas drapers. Ed also made improvements in the knotter system by holding the twine more securely for better knots. The longer bale chamber produced superior bales that attracted farmers' attention. Commercial hay shippers liked the large, well-formed bales. When power-take-off drive tractors became available, New Holland replaced the earlier Wisconsin engine-driven Model 77. This arrangement increased operator safety on hilly ground, making this model even more attractive.

Enthusiastic customers gobbled up the new Model 77 balers leaving many unsold Model 76's languishing at the plant, even when they were offered at a substantial discount! Eventually New Holland gave up selling them, and shipped them off to Europe as part of the Marshall Plan designed to help European Allies recover after World War II. Farmers in England, France, the Netherlands, Germany, and Italy had New Holland balers working in their fields! They were more enchanted with the 76 than their American peers had been. Introduction of the Model 76 paved the way for more New Holland balers abroad in the years to come. Offspring of the Nolt Special was spreading internationally![13]

New Holland didn't rest on its accomplishments. The company continued to look for an edge in the baler business. New manufacturing technology helped make the next baler improvements possible. The company was one of the first to use TIP dies to make highly tooled parts at a lower cost. With these dies, parts could be stamped out of sheet metal without the heavier angle iron supports normally used to strengthen construction.[14]

Making lighter parts with less steel did not diminish performance, and enabled New Holland to sell the Model 66 at a competitive price. While the heavier Model 77 baler was best for custom balers and large farms, this lighter, smaller Model 66 was ideal for most farmers' needs. It could be pulled with a one or two-plow tractor. The smaller, lighter bales appealed to farmers who were handling bales in their daily chores.

President George C. Delp declared the Model 66 to be the most compact baler ever built. Engineers described its pre-compression action as a new principle in baling adding to the machine's capacity. Its gentleness in handling hay saved more leaves, and increased the hay's feeding value. The baler's low center of gravity allowed the farmer to look back over the complete operation from the tractor seat.

Ed introduced another fascinating feature in the Model 66. He eliminated the plunger-stroke delay that had been the signature accomplishment of his first baler. Even though the plunger's speed was increased, the bale-tying mechanism activated so rapidly there was no need to suspend the plunger's operation. The horizontal wad-board added to the baler's compactness. Relocating the knotters on top kept them clear of debris, improving their reliability. The Model 66 gained a reputation for its reliability, affordability and endurance. It was an amazing demonstration of Ed Nolt's team to design outside the box, and was a radical departure from the past. Engineers believed its features represented one of the biggest developments in balers since the automatic pickup baler introduced by New Holland in 1940.[15]

In some ways the Model 66 baler might be considered the high-water mark of Ed's influence and achievements at New Holland. In the future, he continued to refine his baler, but would share more of this responsibility with professional engineers. Mr. Larry Skromme became Chief Engineer in this time of transition. His job was to bring more professional engineers on board, and he would set new standards and protocol for product development. While this signaled declining influence for the blacksmith engineers, they were still an integral part of New Holland.

Mr. Skromme, recognizing Ed Nolt's status within the company, created an office for him in one corner of Ed's shop. He always had a shop where he could work, but the added office was an appropriate recognition of Ed's status, importance to the company, and his desire for privacy.

ED'S ROOM

Known simply as "Ed's room," in the Experimental Department, this was really a shop where he could work. Here his creativity would flourish. Above the office door a sign instructed, "Contact by Phone." This was the company's reminder not to walk into his shop unannounced. Ed wasn't comfortable with "onlookers" who weren't necessary to his work. It was also an indication of his important role in the company. Perhaps Ed didn't appreciate the sign as it called attention to his private nature, but employees like Shaun Seymour weren't affected. They knew how to read Ed and when it was suitable to engage him. If the curtain on his office door was closed, it wasn't a good time for chit chat. His office also provided a place for safekeeping the information he and John Eberly preferred to keep private.

A large overhead door facilitated movement of machinery in and out of the building. People could work at several lathes and other machinery scattered along the shop's walls. Two workbenches faced each other in the middle of the room. Here John Eberly and Ed Nolt worked closely together. They had worked side by side ever since the baler's early days in Farmersville. They didn't always agree on procedures or solutions, and sometimes retreated to a corner of the shop to hash out their differences. To the shop foreman, Bob Steely, John might have been just another employee, but to Ed, he was much more.

Many shop windows provided good lighting for their work and a view of the railroad tracks outside. Looking up from his office desk, Ed could glimpse the baler-laden freight cars just beyond the shop. Observing another shipment leaving the plant by rail, he must have felt some satisfaction; however, it's doubtful that he shared such thoughts with others. But not all of New Holland's baler ventures enjoyed success.[16]

Companies have their successes and failures. Their ability to respond and learn from failures is an important indicator of that company's health and values. For New Holland, the Model 166, self-propelled baler, became one of those difficult trials. Despite the misgivings of Chief Engineer, Larry Skromme, the project was rushed into production. The fact that Ed Nolt didn't work on the project indicates where his sentiments lay. He believed that more time and engineering should have been used before production began.

A favorite lathe in Ed's room. Photo courtesy of Frank N. Weaver.

The Model 166 would be the last of the blacksmith engineer-dominant projects. This was the turning point for the company from blacksmith engineering to professional engineers. To begin large scale production, engineers had to design, test and develop detailed production plans. Although there were still blacksmith engineers at New Holland, professional engineers increased in numbers and influence. Engineering and field testing before production enhanced the New Holland reputation for a quality product.

As the 166 continued to be plagued with difficulties in the field, unhappy customers' complaints grew. Finally, to protect the integrity of the New Holland brand, and its reputation for a quality product, the company bought back all but two of the troublesome balers. It had been a most difficult experience, but the company learned much.

President Delp decreed there would be no more self-propelled balers, and recognized that Mr. Skromme's lack of support had been well founded. With Larry Skromme's leadership, professional engineers would chart the future.

The ill-fated Model 166 self-propelled baler didn't meet New Holland's standards of reliability and quality products.

Ed Nolt wasn't happy with this shift to professional engineers, but quality control and mass production made it necessary. Although the baler was still king, Ed was disappointed that his input would now be limited to baler development. Other product lines would be engineered without consulting him. Bob Ressler shared Ed's concern, and emphatically challenged the need for engineers! The human resources department took over responsibilities for hiring, and completed the shift to professional engineers.

Ed expressed some of his frustration about professional engineers during the testing of an irrigation system at the pond below his home. The system, designed by engineers, didn't work. Ed exclaimed that if he had been the one to blame, there would have been much more fuss! [17]

MERGER WITH THE SPERRY CORPORATION

New Holland's merger with the Sperry Corporation, known as Sperry New Holland, was another significant juncture for New Holland's future. It was the first step of New Holland's passing from a successful, small-town company into a succession of mergers with global implications. The merger brought more operating capital and plant expansion making it possible to meet the increasing demand for balers that would only escalate within the stability and security of its new corporate status.

In 1947 the Sperry Corporation acquired New Holland as part of its diversification program's plan to stabilize postwar income. During World War II the company prospered, producing gyro-compasses, radar components, airplane controls and hydraulics. But in peacetime, demand for such products dropped, and profits with it. In its drive to diversify, Sperry became a major conglomerate of the postwar period. New Holland was an attractive acquisition for Sperry. Ed Peters reported its sales had grown from $100,000.00 in 1940 to over $27,000,000.00 by 1947. [18]

In 1955 Sperry and Remington Rand merged to become the Sperry Rand Corporation. Other subsidiaries of New Holland, Hertzler and Zook, Dellinger Manufacturing, and Smoker Farm Elevators, also became part of this local Sperry Rand division. Other mergers and acquisitions would follow encompassing New Holland into an ever-widening corporate blend.

New Holland realized postwar competition would soon be a reality as other farm equipment manufacturers switched to peacetime production. There were two things New Holland needed to stay ahead of its competition: operating capital and product creativity. Henry Fisher was in his element with the financial challenges, and Ed Nolt's creativity was an asset to engineering's tasks—one aspect of this merger not easily quantified on paper.

New Holland needed operating capital to expand production and to establish a dealer credit system. The merger enabled the company to move away from its early cash-and-carry days. Sperry's financial resources allowed New Holland to expand its physical plant as demand for product increased dramatically. Sperry ruled that some profits would be invested in advertising and engineering's development of future products. While this meant less money for shareholders, it was money well spent, benefitting both Sperry and New Holland.

Perhaps neither Sperry or New Holland realized at the time of the merger just how much they would benefit. Ed Nolt's extremely popular Model 66 baler was put into production in 1953. The company forecast 3,000 balers could be sold the first year, but this prediction was soon overrun by weekly increases in demand. Ivan Glick describes the situation: "In near panic, additional assembly lines for pickups and other assemblies were set up for a total of night and day manufacturing [at the] rate of six to eleven minutes per baler. For Sperry, it was like having a license to print money."[19] During the years of the popular Model 66, New Holland modified its familiar red color, painting the baler pickups a bright yellow. Red and yellow became the iconic colors of the New Holland line.

Due to his work at New Holland, Ed's name became familiar at the United States' Patent Office as frequent patent applications crossed the desk of an examiner, Mr. Stone, who followed these applications with interest. Stone was fascinated with Ed's work and background. He wanted to meet him. Mr. Stone invited Ed to visit the patent office in Washington, D.C. With his accustomed reserve, Nolt declined the invitation, but could not refuse the next request—if Mr. Stone came to New Holland, could he meet with Ed? Upon receiving an affirmative answer, eight patent examiners made the trip to New Holland! Over the period of his lifetime, Ed was granted more than 50 patents, most of them pertaining to his baler.[20]

Ed Nolt didn't get lost in this process of corporate expansion and integration. While he would have felt like a fish out of water in the wheeling and dealing of markets and mergers, he was quite content to continue his innovative work on his baler along with his design team. New Holland's patent attorney, Joseph A. Brown, wrote:

> Ed was not a one-shot inventor. He had a creative mind. Inventions flowed from him. He was an invaluable asset to New Holland. Combined with his design group of Otto Luek, Jim McDuffie, [and Pete Sturla], New Holland had a world-class team that progressed with each engineering success. It was like a baseball team having three 20-game winning pitchers…The red and yellow machine became well-known, the standard of the industry, the benchmark from which all other balers were measured.[21]

Title	Application Number
Means for baling material	201,089
Hydraulically controlled baler	533,415
Conveyor for hay gathering and feeding mechanism	525,787
Automatic slack take-up mechanism	268,950
Bale tension regulator	301,863
Finger Feed Conveyors	429,761
Double twist wire tie mechanism	341,056
Two-spool Needle-borne tier	341,055
Hay baler wire tying mechanism	388,132
Hay Balers	268,424
Adjustable wind-guard for baler pick-up	567,342
Hay Baler	648,526
hay baler	750,492
Safeth device for tier needles	76,207
Safety Device	10,646
Hay Baler	86,765
Hay Baler	93,541
Hay Baler	66,288
Hay Baler	256,576
Bait Chummer	403,060
Knotter Bill Hook	633,496
Guide for Knotter Needle of Baler	661,017
Twine finger and actuating means for baler	661,014
Knotter clamp means for baler	660,967
Twine Clamping Means and Cutter for Baler	660,968
Twine finger for knotter mechanism of baler	661,033
Hay Baler	543,845
Gear housing for tier assembly of baler	661,096
Hay Baler	641,553
Hay Baler	641,551
Twine clamp means for baler knotter	739,085
Needle Actuated Twine Guide for Baler Knotter	752,875
Twine tensioning attachment	713,944
Knotter mechanism having a twine guide cooperating with a bill hook	188,409
Knotter mechanism	10,205
Knot tying mechanism	10,206
Anchoring apparatus	298,697

A partial list of Ed's patents. Nolt family collection.

CHAPTER 5 *"It Changed Everything"*

Millersville professor, Richard Beam, interviewed Harry Stauffer, a long-time Farmersville resident, on his 85th birthday. The interview, conducted in Pennsylvania German, was printed in the *Ephrata Review*. Stauffer shared many interesting memories of village life and the changes he had witnessed during his lifetime. He noted Ed Nolt's invention as one of the major events of the neighborhood. Asked it he had ever owned one of Ed's balers, Stauffer replied, "no", but he said when Ed invented his baler, *"Das hot alles verrenert"* (that changed everything)! Indeed it had in ways that took Ed's baler far from home.[1]

The fledgling company reorganized in 1940 found its wings with the Nolt baler. It grew through its merger with the Sperry Corporation. Acquisition of the first European self-propelled Claeys combine was another step of growth. In 1986 Ford purchased Sperry New Holland. In 1991, Fiat merged with Ford New Holland, and in 1995 it became known as New Holland North America. Today New Holland Agricultural and New Holland Construction are two divisions of CNH International. New Holland is the North American headquarters for both divisions. Ed Nolt's baler begun in his Farmersville barn, the reorganized New Holland Company, and small-town New Holland are now globally connected!

While much had changed for New Holland over the years,

A present-day photo depicting the distance travelled from Farmersville to today. Note the round baler in the background and the street named George C. Delp. Delp guided New Holland Machine into the modern era from its humble beginnings. Photo by author.

things had changed for Ed too. Not only had Ed Nolt found a solution to his threshing problem, it had become much more. Now far from his winter shop and its humble beginning, the success of Ed's baler presented an unimagined dilemma—Ed Nolt had become a wealthy man!

During his retirement years, Ed accompanied two grandsons, Kenneth and Michael Burkholder, to the popular Peoples' Restaurant in downtown New Holland. Ken remembers that as they enjoyed their meal together, Ed looked up at the lunch counter seats and recalled how he had routinely eaten there with President George Delp and other New Holland men. It was one of the ways Ed had become accustomed to life in the corporate world. His Farmersville contemporaries would rarely, if ever, have considered such a luxury in that era, but for Ed it had become commonplace.

GEORGE C. DELP: CONFIDANT

One of the unique benefits Ed Nolt had at New Holland was the fatherly financial advice of George Delp. Perhaps in today's terms this relationship could be described as the best fringe benefit Ed Nolt enjoyed as part of the company.

While financial management wasn't Ed's strong suit, George Delp had his back. This is best illustrated by the spirit and detailed, frank advice George Delp gave to Ed in a 1956 letter. In the letter, Mr. Delp explained Ed Nolt's 1955 tax return. The eight page single spaced letter commented on the general state of Ed's financial affairs, gifting, tax strategies, estate planning and other issues. Ed and Mr. Delp had a special bond of trust. Their ability to converse in Ed's preferred Pennsylvania Dutch strengthened their relationship. This yearly review allowed Ed to keep his focus on his work without the distractions of money management.

In the letter, Mr. Delp reassures Ed that he has no reason to be concerned about overspending. He writes: "…quite frankly, I think your position is exactly the reverse. For a person of your means, you are inclined to live much more frugally than would be the desire of most people." He goes on to suggest that Ed feel free to use more of his money for things he would like to do for himself and others.[2]

While acknowledging Ed had the right to use his money as he chose, Delp expressed pointed concern about the number of mortgages and other personal loans Ed was making. He advised Ed to avoid making such personal loans, and encouraged him to establish loans on a business-like basis of secured loans and recorded mortgages.

With Landis Buchen's passing in 1955, Delp proposed that Clarence Nelson take over the management of these notes and mortgages, and become the general manager of Nolt's finances under Mr. Delp's supervision. He also observed that personal loan requests made to Ed could be directed to Mr. Nelson for consideration on a less personal basis than had been the case with Ed and Landis Buchen. Hopefully dealing with Mr. Nelson would reduce the number of requests.

The most difficult problem according to Geroge Delp, was that too many people were still making personal requests of Ed for money, and George asserted this is a matter that "you alone must control." He saw Nelson as one who could look out for Ed's interests and yet honor any specific requests Ed made if he desired to assist someone financially.

As with other letters to Nolt explaining financial matters or royalty payments, Mr. Delp encouraged Ed to ask any questions if he has concerns. He ends the letter writing: "Again I would like to say that it is our desire to help you just as much as we can, and to relieve you to the extent possible of any details which you would like to avoid."[3]

The company established a post office box to receive dividend and other checks for processing by Clarence Nelson without needing to bother Ed. If Ed desired, it was suggested that Nelson could also write checks for Ed, but here Ed appears to have drawn the line regarding such an arrangement. Mr. Delp supports the wisdom of Ed's desire to remain in the loop, writing, "We do not want to suggest for a moment that you have someone else handle anything which you would like to handle yourself. Our only desire is to relieve you of items from which you desire relief and to help you as much as possible."[4]

Periodically, Mr. Delp also sent Ed dispersement voucher letters summarizing baler sales with the list of serial numbers in neatly typed rows, total sales and Ed's royalties for that period. True to Delp's style, the letters are concise and businesslike with a spirit of cordiality between equal partners in a prospering relationship. New Holland's honoring of this long-established, lucrative royalty agreement was admirable by today's business standards. In today's corporate world, Ed Nolt would likely have been shunted aside in some fashion. New Holland was smart enough to recognize that together they had a good thing going![5]

George Delp's financial assistance was an invaluable asset to Ed in the corporate world. It freed him from financial details he hoped to avoid to work in his shop. But in addition to the financial aspects, Mr. Delp helped Ed navigate the corporate culture so foreign to his upbringing. As illustrated by the Peoples' Restaurant story, Delp helped Ed hold together these two worlds—corporate America and his Mennonite farm community background.[6]

While during his whole life frugality remained instinctive to Ed, his lifestyle did reflect his changing situation, and Mr. Delp's encouragement to enjoy some of the fruits of his well-deserved labors.

One of Ed's diversions was the restoration of Stanley Steamer automobiles. As a young boy, Ammon Zimmerman remembers Ed showing up at Zimmerman's Steel Shop in a Stanley Steamer and giving some rides. Ammon concluded that Ed had his playthings, but he could have "played" a lot more when compared to other men of such means.

Ed took pleasure in hunting and fishing on his boat. He wasn't reluctant to spend money for the latest and best technology in mechanical things that fascinated him. This included things such as cars, boats and home appliances.

He enjoyed exploring the new technology of his automobiles. On one occasion he filled the car with engineers to test the new Oldsmobile's air bag suspension on some rough road. He wanted to see if the suspension lived up to its billing.

When ordering new cars from the local Sauder dealership, Ed often wanted equipment that sales people said wasn't available. Ed learned to connect directly with engineers in Detroit to work things out. They developed a working relationship regarding his special needs.[7]

By the 1950's, the large amounts of royalty checks arriving at the Nolt household must have been astounding to Annie and Ed, and the accumulating wealth difficult to comprehend. Not everyone appreciated Ed's financial situation. Recently when asked if she was related to Ed Nolt, the daughter of a distant relative's first words were, "The millionaire?" While she didn't personally know him, she said that her father called Ed a "tightwad." Perhaps the Clarence Nelson buffer was paying off, and Ed was less ready to make the personal loans George Delp discouraged. What many didn't know was how much Ed was sharing his wealth for others benefit.

In 1947, a major loan from Ed made it possible for Ephrata to begin construction of its new community hospital. Landis Buchen, Ed's financial advisor at that time, was awarded a $410,000 contract to build the new Ephrata Community Hospital. A later article about construction of the new hospital described Ed's role as follows: "Edwin B. Nolt of the thriving New Holland Machine Company held a note for $200,000." While this was not an outright gift, it did help make the project's beginning possible. Ed would soon go beyond wise investments finding another way to use his growing wealth.[8]

AN EMBARRASSMENT OF RICHES—TOO MUCH OF A GOOD THING?

The story is told of a day when Ed and Anna visited Ebersole's Chair Shop looking for new chairs. After finding some that would adequately meet their needs, Ed looked at some higher quality, more expensive chairs he preferred. When Annie voiced reservations about the added cost, Ed reportedly replied they could buy them, and the chairs would be paid for by all those "red things" going down the train tracks. Others also remember seeing those solid lines of railroad cars loaded with red balers departing on their journey from New Holland to Lancaster and points way beyond this small town. The cost of a few chairs was minuscule.[9]

The continued royalties from all those "red things" indeed made the chair expense a small matter. But as the wealth continued to multiply, Anna felt they had enough and hoped the royalties could be stopped. Ed's response was that they should just let them come for a while. The story illustrates Ed's belief in just compensation. On one hand increasing wealth was troubling and brought its own problems; on the other hand, cutting it off didn't seem like the right thing to do. The biblical injunction that a worker rightly deserves his wages might also have influenced Ed's thinking. Better to be a good steward responsible for income justly earned than to turn it away. But no matter how generous Ed became with his wealth—largely unknown to many—there was the price of social distance that could be felt, even if only from the envious!

One of the troubling realities of wealth was the Nolt's concern for their children's safety. After the family moved to New Holland, their children didn't walk the rural road to school, they were driven by a family member. Memories of the Lindbergh family's tragedy still lingered in the public mind. Their story raised the perils of fame and fortune that didn't escape the Nolts.

In 1927, Charles A. Lindbergh gained instant world fame by flying his "Spirit of St. Louis" solo, non-stop across the Atlantic Ocean to Paris, France. Five years later the Lindbergh's baby son, Charles Jr., was taken from his bedroom crib at night. Although a ransom note demanding money was left behind, baby Charles was murdered by his abductors. This story's unhappy ending was a cautionary tale regarding wealth and fame—perhaps another reason Ed preferred to keep a low profile—it was a reminder that the wealthy sometimes become the victims of their own good fortune.[10]

Despite his wealth, Ed never forgot who he was or the people he belonged to. Whenever there was a financial need in his congregation, Ed gave freely. The church assisted members suffering significant financial loss due to fire, hospitalization or other emergencies. After assessing the situation, a congregational free will offering assisted those in need. When this didn't raise the necessary funds, Ed gave more to meet the shortfall. On one occasion when a relative was hospitalized, Ed simply informed the hospital that he would pay the bill. Privately he was generous with his money and responded to the needs of others, but this didn't satisfy everyone.

Near the end of his life, Ed confided to a relative that he felt some people didn't seem to like him.[11] The "millionaire" label troubled him. It threatened to separate him from his ordinary beginnings and lifestyle still assumed at the core of his identity. In reality, Ed remained grounded in who he had always been, but he looked to others to help him find a way out of this predicament. Again, George Delp was standing by, ready to help.

THE CRELS FOUNDATION

When Ed Nolt announced his intention to make a baler that really worked, he couldn't have imagined the amount of wealth that eventually came his way. His boyhood shop tinkering had grown to define him. What his mother surmised in his early years had come to pass—he just wasn't a farmer at heart, but she didn't need to worry. Following his heart, he would find his way and develop his potential in a very different direction.

The success of Ed's baler had people talking. The raspberries of the boys over the failures at his Farmersville garage had faded long ago, but perhaps still lingered in his psyche. Now the talk was about Ed's wealth. But Ed didn't relish this anymore than the boys' previous kidding. He confided to George Delp, "They're saying I'm a millionaire. I don't want to be a millionaire. I want to give my money away, so they can't say I'm a millionaire." President George Delp and others listened as Ed shared his concerns. The company that had made him wealthy was ready to help. They assisted him in working through complicated issues regarding income, taxes and philanthropic possibilities.[12]

Robert G. LaTourneau's private foundation became a model for the New Holland group. LaTourneau was a very successful Christian businessman who reversed church teaching of a 10 percent tithe that many churches taught. Instead he gave away 90 percent of his income and lived on 10 percent. Work began enabling Ed to follow LaTourneau's example.[13]

The solution to honor Ed's wishes was the establishment of a private foundation that became known as the CRELS Foundation. Using the initials of the tax law classifying charitable foundations—

NEW HOLLAND OPERATING GROUP

INTER OFFICE CORRESPONDENCE

TO: Mr. G. C. Delp
FROM:
SUBJECT:

January 12, 1950

Dear George:

    I am willing to continue the baler royalty payment situation which, at your request, I started with Ed, if that is what you would like me to do and I think the letter you dictated January 21 covers the situation quite well.

    It seems to me, however, that this letter to Ed should be signed by you as an officer of the company rather than by me — therefore, if you would like me to continue the matter with Ed and the attached letter meets with your approval, I am willing to try to do so.

                  Very truly yours,

                    J. H. Fisher

JHF:ADK
Enclosure
131

Letter from J. H. Fisher to George Delp consenting to continue the royalty agreement between New Holland Machine and Ed Nolt. The continuation of this agreement later served to provide the funding for the CRELS Foundation. Nolt family collection.

"Charitable, Religious, Educational, Literary, and Scientific"—the CRELS foundation was born. Ed served as a foundation trustee, determined the amount to be contributed each year, and worked with the board to determine recipients of the foundation's grants. He favored grants to hospitals, nursing homes, parochial Mennonite schools, and the Horning Mennonite Church.

During the complex discussions regarding the tax laws and proceedings needed to establish his foundation, Ed would sometimes appear to be asleep. However, when George Delp asked Ed for his thoughts on the matter being discussed, Ed's response indicated he was listening and understood what was happening. Clarence Nelson was amazed at Ed's ability to understand these complicated details. It was apparent that while Ed preferred to live in his mechanical world, he did understand the financial world and details he preferred to leave to others he trusted. This arrangement at New Holland was a great blessing enabling Ed to pursue his mechanical muse unencumbered by financial issues.[14]

Ed was instrumental in the foundation of the Fairmount Homes, a Retirement Community located a few miles from his birthplace. Photo by author.

In his role as board chair of two, one-room Mennonite schools, Farmersville and Shaffers, Luke Weaver has received checks from the CRELS Foundation. When he returned the foundation's required report form, he added a personal thank you note saying that some of Ed Nolt's money had come back to the house where Ed grew up as a teenager! The Weavers now live on the former Nolt farm.

As might be expected, Ed declined to have the Nolt family name attached to the foundation, but family members do serve as board trustees. At its beginning, there were no press releases to publicize the CRELS arrangement, and not many people knew about Ed's philanthropy.

The 2014 CRELS report shows the significance of this foundation today. Every year for the past 27 years it has distributed approximately 5 percent of average assets. In 1955 this amounted to $20,000.00, in 1994 the amount was $397,000.00, and in 2004, $743,000.00. In 2014 the CRELS foundation gave grants totaling $990,000.00.[15]

George Delp also urged Ed to establish trust funds for his children as Delp himself had done. Ed and wife, Anna, demurred revealing some insights of their concerns regarding wealth. What was best in making provisions for the children? Reflecting on his own life as a young man, Ed wondered what would have happened to him if he had suddenly inherited a large amount of money. In the end, he did take Delp's advice in making provisions for their children.[16]

Today, traveling towards Farmersville, in the distance one can see the prominent buildings of a retirement center on the ridge of Fairmount Hill above Farmersville. *Katze Boucle Weeg* (Cat's Back Road) intersects the ridge cutting the Fairmount Homes center in half, east and west. Fairmount was the dream of Ed's sister, Katie, who asked Ed for help. Ed Nolt funded half the initial cost of Fairmount. Although he could have paid for all of it, he believed others should share some of the responsibility for its funding. Below Fairmount Hill, there is a bare field where Ed's barn-shop and house stood, but for those who knew about Ed, it is a reminder of this significant gift from a local farm boy to his Farmersville community.[17]

1953

CLARENCE J. NELSON

September 23, 1995

Mr. Kenneth Burkholder

During our conversation this morning, you indicated that it would be helpful to you if I were to share my recollection of events that led to the establishment of the Crels Foundation, and other matters having to do with your grandfather. You also indicated that you thought your brothers would share that interest. I am addressing this memorandum to you and you may share it as you see fit.

My position at New Holland Machine Company was somewhat unique. I was employed as an accountant by J. Paul Lyet, officially the Controller. However, he was more than the Controller due to the management technique employed by George C. Delp, President. George Delp was a prolific worker who surrounded himself with capable people, and then played on the talents of those persons in a manner much like an orchestra leader directs the musicians who make up his organization.

Although I was employed as an Accountant, working under J. Paul Lyet, I soon found that I was working equally for George C. Delp. I wrote letters, etc., for both of them (in addition to my other duties). Amusingly, there were times when they were arguing between themselves about something, by written correspondence, and I was in the unique position of composing the letters representing the thinking of both.

The foregoing is intended to explain how I became a party to the events that led to the formation of the Crels Foundation. Ed Nolt was paying one of his occasional visits to George Delp's office, and both Paul Lyet and I were called in to participate in the conference. J. H. Fisher may have been there, also, although my memory is not clear on that point.

Of course, there is some prior history of importance. Ed Nolt had been employed by New Holland when arrangements were made to take a license under his baler patent. His salary was $50.00 per week, and he never received a raise in that rate of compensation. He did receive a royalty based on the total sales of balers. Paul Lyet, in his responsibility as Financial officer of New Holland, decided that the company's position would be more secure if the Company was the owner of the patent, rather than just a licensee. As the result of his efforts, an agreement was made whereby Ed sold his patent to the company under an arrangement where the sales price would be based on baler sales through the life of the patent.

As it turned out, this action was vital to Ed's prosperity. If he had received royalties over the years, they would have been taxed as ordinary income and, at that time, the highest tax bracket was in the 75% area. But a patent was considered to be a Capital Asset

The history of the CRELS Foundation as documented by Clarence J. Nelson. Nolt family collection.

and its sale was a capital transaction. Therefore, the proceeds were taxed as capital gain income at a maximum rate of 25%. The Internal Revenue Service challenged the capital gain concept, taking the position that the proceeds were based on sales and constituted a royalty. It was this contest that led to obtaining the services of a prominent Washington law firm, and tax expert Thomas J. Beddow. Tom Beddow spearheaded this matter through the Internal Revenue Service to a successful conclusion. This result added greatly to the financial status of Edwin B. Nolt.

With this background, you can sympathize with Ed's thinking as he came to the office that day and complained "People are talking about me." "What are they saying about you, Ed?" "They are saying I am a millionaire. I don't want to be a millionaire. I want to give my money away, so they can't say I am a millionaire." This led to a general discussion and a decision to delay any action until we could think things through, and determine the best course of action to accomplish Ed's objective. In view of the major help already received from Tom Beddow, it was decided to ask his advice.

Tom came back with a proposal to establish a Private Foundation. This idea was prompted by a special law enacted for the benefit of Robert G. LeTourneau. Bob LeTourneau was also an inventor and a very successful businessman. He was a Christian and a practicing tither. When he prospered, he set aside the tithe as the Lord's portion, but decided that was not a fair division. "It would be more proper to give the Lord 90% and keep 10% for myself. God helping me, that is what I will do." And he did.

LeTourneau's practice came to the attention of a member of Congress. At that time, the tax deduction for charitable contributions was limited to 30% of Adjusted Gross Income. Therefore, Bob LeTourneau was giving 90% but was able to deduct only 30%. It appears this probably continued for eight or more years. The law passed by Congress provided that, if a person pays out in charitable contributions and federal income taxes a total of 90% of his Adjusted Gross Income, and has done so for eight of the last ten years, he would be entitled to an unlimited charitable deduction (up to his actual contributions) for that year.

Tom's recommendation was that we embark on a program to qualify under that law, meeting the 90% requirement for eight years, so Ed could, thereafter, deduct his full contributions. He recommended the formation of a charitable foundation as the primary vehicle by which to accomplish that overall objective. Tom came to New Holland and met with us to explain all of this. Agreement was readily reached and Tom was commissioned to write the instrument to establish the Foundation.

The next question was a name for the foundation. Ed declined to have his name used when others suggested it be the "Nolt Foundation". "New Holland Foundation" would give the wrong impression. After much discussion, it was agreed to use the initials of the tax law classification of charitable foundations, "Charitable, Religious, Educational, Literary, and Scientific". We played with those five initials, even having the computer print out every possible combination, and, possibly, adding an "A" between numbers four and five. This led to CRESAL and other similar possibilities, and we decided on CRELS.

On December 26, 1953, a meting was held to execute the agreement and thus get the Foundation under way in that year by making an initial contribution. I was on vacation that week and was called in for the meeting, as it was a priority matter. It was decided that Ed Nolt, George Delp and J. H. Fisher would be the initial trustees (who would serve for life and would each have the power to designate a successor upon their death or retirement.) It was further agreed that J. Paul Lyet, II, and Clarence J. Nelson would be elected to serve for one year at a time. George C. Delp was elected Chairman and I was elected Secretary.

In my capacity as Secretary, I handled administrative matters, the accounting, and the preparation of tax returns. It was also my responsibility to make certain that Ed's affairs were handled so as to make certain he qualified under the law by making the required contributions each year to meet the 90% figure for the combination of contributions and income taxes. We were trying to build the history of eight years so as to qualify for an unlimited deduction in the ninth year.

Meanwhile, the original patent expired. Under the agreement with Ed, all patents obtained after he was employed by New Holland automatically became the property of New Holland. Therefore, New Holland had no obligation to Ed other than the $50.00 per week stipend. But that was not a satisfactory arrangement. New Holland wanted Ed to have an incentive to continue to invent improvements and new models, so a deal was made for him to continue to receive a percentage of baler sales. The I. R. S. said this arrangement was clearly a royalty and the proceeds were taxable as ordinary income, and Ed's tax returns were filed on that basis.

But we were still dealing with Tom Beddow who was our legal expert relative to the Foundation. Along the way, it was decided to file an appeal to the I.R.S. position, and Tom handled that through to its conclusion. It was another victory. By that time we had qualified for eight consecutively years and were ready to enjoy the unlimited deduction. However, the successful result of the tax claim had produced a windfall rebate and it was, therefore, decided to elect to not qualify in that year. The following year we did qualify and, of course, also had the history of having qualified over eight of the preceding ten years.

Each year, we would have a meeting with Ed and Katie to determine the Crels distribution for the year, the amount Ed would contribute that year to the Foundation, and other matters having to do with Ed's financial affairs. Ed had some definite ideas with respect to the contributions, although more often they were negative rather than positive. The Mennonite Central Committee rated high priority at the outset but fell into disfavor along the way. The same was true of Eastern Mennonite College. Presumably, those changes in attitude had to do with reaction to a degree of liberalism. On the other hand, he readily went along with recommendations made by other Trustees, even though some of them were foreign to his thinking. For instance, we made contributions to Philhaven Hospital and, on one occasion, he reacted negatively to giving something to it. I suggested to him that, while there may be something in their administration to which he reacted negatively, I suspected the same and worse was true of some of the other beneficiaries of Crels' gifts. He thought about that, chuckled a bit, and agreed to continue with Philhaven.

From the beginning, Ed was favorable to medical institutions, including nursing homes, parochial Mennonite schools, and the Horning Mennonite Church

As you know, when J. H. Fisher died, John H. Frey was elected a Trustee. J. Paul Lyet died and Katie Nolt became a Trustee. John Frey died. This led to consideration of various possibilities relative to the future of Crels. Ed had provided that there should always be a lineal descendent on the Board and it was decided that the best way of carrying out his wishes would be to give the Board a distinctive "Nolt" flavor. Consequently, we now have three of his grandsons serving as Trustees, leaving only Delp and Nelson from the original Board, and both of them are now octogenarians. The future is up to you and your brothers.

George Delp (and his associated team of Fisher, Lyet, and Nelson) were involved as advisors and administrators of much of Ed's affairs in addition to the Crels association. For instance, George Delp was the prime mover is encouraging Ed to establish trusts for his children. He had done so for his own children and considered it desirable from a tax saving point of view. Ed was not convinced, nor was his wife, Anna. I remember Ed saying " I don't know what would have happened to me if I had been given a quarter million dollars when I was a young person". Nevertheless, George prevailed and the trusts were established for Clarence, Vera, and Edwin. The one for Shirley was instigated by Ed and Katie, who wanted her to be treated equally with the others.

Somewhere along the way, I took over the bookkeeping for Ed and Katie, while John Frey handled that for the children. My duties kept me in close association with Ed and Katie, for whom I held the utmost respect. I didn't know Anna very well as she was pretty much an invalid from the time of my first association. She would be sitting on the lawn but very limited in energy. She had a sweet personality which I much admired.

From my perspective Ed and Katie had a fine marriage. Katie accepted her role and Ed greatly appreciated all she did. There was a significant difference in ages but I did not observe any great problems stemming therefrom. Katie, naturally, wanted to be a mother and both of them agreed to accept a foster child to meet that desire... Ed and Katie wanted Shirley to be treated as nearly as possible as the others.

I visited Ed and Katie on one occasion in Florida because of the need to get their signatures on a State Equipment document. I was shown the fishing boat, and visited Katie at the Nursing Home where she was then working. It was a glimpse into the lives of two people providentially brought together and enjoying the lifestyles that they preferred and in which they felt most comfortable.

While Ed preferred mechanical interests to financial and paperwork details, I was often amazed by his understanding of complicated details. I think of an occasion when we were dealing with a very involved tax matter with experts Tom Beddow and Joe Hecht of the Ernst and Ernst Accounting firm. Ed had his eyes closed and looked to be asleep. George turned to him and said, "Ed, what do you think?" Ed opened his eyes and made a statement that showed he was fully aware of the situation under discussion. On another occasion, we were in an Engineering Review meeting at Sperry New Holland, and the subject was a new baler model being developed by other engineers in the organization. Ed was napping, and was startled when George called on him for comment. He did so in one brief sentence "There is going to be an awful lot of vibration in that design". The new baler was introduced and failed because of excess vibration.

That pretty much sums up the highpoints. If there are other specific matters on which you would like me to comment, I will try to summon them to memory.

Sincerely,

Clarence
Clarence J. Nelson

CHAPTER 6 *The Later Years*

Ed appeared to mellow somewhat as he grew older, to let down his guard and enjoy some of life's pleasures. Despite the strong work ethic of his upbringing, he found ways to play—plowing snow and fishing on his boat. Ed's boat reportedly had a sign that read, "The only difference between men and boys is the size of their toys." Whether plowing snow or fishing, Ed's toys were big!

GONE FISHING!

Ed had a boat on the Conestoga River in the family's early years at Farmersville. Family members remember enjoying time spent together on the Conestoga and the Chesapeake Bay. Later in life Ed learned to enjoy fishing. After moving to New Holland, he had a boat built to his specifications. He ordered two large marine engines for the boat and had them shipped to Lancaster. When notified that the engines had arrived, he was eager to keep the project going. He headed for Lancaster with a New Holland company truck and driver.

Upon arrival at the freight company's loading dock, he identified his engines but apparently the crew wasn't impressed by his appearance—usually dressed in greasy, well-worn bib overalls—claiming such highly expensive freight seemed unlikely. They refused to load his engines. Without making a scene, Ed quietly went off in search of someone higher up in authority. In the meantime, the New Holland driver told the dock crew who this man was, and suggested they better get ready to load the engines. True to the driver's prediction, when Ed returned, his engines were loaded and he was on his way.[1]

Ed enjoyed his boat's powerful engines, and he was always in a hurry to get to his fishing spot. As he often said, he wanted to get there before all the fish were gone! Frequently when he was ready to move to a new area he took off under full power. Men fishing on the stern had to hang on for dear life or be thrown overboard. A family member also remembers such mischievousness. Ed, with a toothpick bobbing in his mouth, only laughed at the sight of people hanging on in such situations. He enjoyed being on the bay. This was a place he could relax and savor. When things weren't going well at the shop, George Delp encouraged Ed to get away from his work and go fishing. Ed said he did some of his best thinking while fishing.

He was careful choosing who went along on these expeditions. He was there to fish. It was not a setting for serious discussions, just fishing. His boat was a unique place where everything, in this era before cell phones, could be left behind. For him, the Chesapeake Bay was a peaceful place of solitude and relaxation with his closest friends. It was special to be on board, and to fish with Ed— sometimes just the ride was worth it!

On one memorable fishing trip, Ed noticed the bay patrol stopping Phares Rutt's boat for some suspected infraction. Curious for a better look, Ed steered closer to the patrol boat and its quarry. He soon realized his presence wasn't appreciated when an officer with a bullhorn yelled, "Get out of here!" Gladly complying, Ed powered up and was soon on his way when he noticed the patrol boat appeared to be coming after him. He told the group not to look back as he hit full throttle. His powerful engines not only got him to his fishing spots in a hurry, he soon discouraged those in pursuit to give up the chase. He was simply following their orders to "get going!" However, the Coast Guard eventually followed Ed's speedy craft to the dock and turned the boat upside down searching for smuggled drugs. Nothing was found except possibly a few good cigars![2]

Ed's catch of the day!

Grandpa Edwin B. Nolt's boat Mitzy *custom built with an aluminum hull and two V8 Cat engines on the Gulf of Mexico docked at Nokomis Beach, FL. Nolt family photos.*

But even in this place of leisure, Ed's inventive mind found projects that challenged him. When fishing at Rock Hall, Ed looked for ways to make tasks easier. One of his most notable projects on the bay was his fish chummer. The chummer ground up fish parts and soft-shell clams creating a slime used to attract fish. After a few short-notice trips with Ed to work on the chummer, engineer Shaun Seymour kept a "gofer bag" under his desk at New Holland. When Ed called, he was ready to go. Although this had the appearance of a few nice days of vacation on the water, Shaun said working on the chummer to create 50 gallons of fish slop really included messy clothes with a distinct smell! The project was a success. It eliminated the need to hire a deckhand to create the chum. Commercial fishermen on the bay bought about 1,500 of Ed's machines.

New Holland sold its chummer line to Frank N. Weaver who had worked at New Holland for several years in the Service Department and Experimental Engineering shops. Frank and Ed got to know each other while both were in Experimental. After leaving New Holland, his company manufactured motorized feed carts known as The Weaverline. He produced the chummer until 1972 when Hurricane Agnes' floodwaters and silt choked the soft-shell clam beds in the Chesapeake Bay. This ended the supply of cheap clams needed for chumming, and demand for the chummer.[3]

While wintering in Florida, Ed enjoyed catching the Florida Grouper. He soon discovered restauranteurs there were eager to purchase these fish at the docks. It was grueling, time-consuming work reeling in a grouper from the depths of the sea. Ed found a solution. He would build an electric powered reel to do his hard work efficiently. Granddaughter Julia Burkholder remembers that while honeymooning in Florida, she used one of Ed's power reels. After pushing a button to turn it on, she said its high torque made it necessary to hang on tight to the rod.

With the power reel Ed believed he could catch his limit of groupers and sell them for enough cash to pay for his boat fuel! He

ALLAN W. SHIRK

NEW HOLLAND
Chummer
World's first automatic chumming machine

Now you can cut and drop chum automatically— even when fish are being played

The Electric Fish Chummer. Ed saw the chore of bait (chum) preparation to be a hard job and one that required an extra deckhand. Ed's solution to this hard work, and the prospect of one less deckhand to pay, was his electric chumming machine.

Ed's Chummer—note the NH Logo as this invention was manufactured and sold by New Holland Machine.

The Electric Fishing Rod. Since grouper are bottom dwellers and quite a chore to bring in, Ed determined that he could boat more fish if he just had a powered reel. Ed was always looking for a technological edge.

asked his fishing buddies to share some of their groupers with him as the only payment necessary for the trip. It was another example of Ed's thrifty, inventive mind at work.

32-lb. catch of the day. Nolt family photos.

Now fishing wasn't just the amusement of idle men as some might have perceived, it was a justifiable pastime!

Another small incident on a fishing trip demonstrated Ed's ingrained thriftiness. The men stopped for bags of ice near Rock Hall. As they loaded the bags, one dropped to the ground spilling ice everywhere. Ed tried to salvage as much of the ice as possible. Watching Ed, one of his buddies observed that if he had Ed's money he would have simply bought another bag! Wealth hadn't changed Ed.

One side benefit for Shaun Seymour on these bay expeditions was that Ed usually paid for their meals and they always ate well!

While Ed willingly paid the bill, Shaun noticed he was less than generous with his tipping—a reflection of his Lancaster County upbringing and frugality. After they discussed the importance of a good tip as part of a server's income, Ed became more charitable, but he still calculated the proper percentage down to the penny!

LAWN SPRINKLERS

Several years after Frank Weaver began manufacturing feed carts, he got a call from Ed Nolt. He inquired if Frank could adapt one of his motorized feed carts for Ed's use. He wanted to use it to transport sprinkler hoses for his lawn irrigation system. An underground system to water the lawn was probably considered a luxury in those days. Frank modified one of his carts and delivered it to Ed at his New Holland home. When tested on the paved driveway, Ed was pleased with the cart's performance and wrote Frank a check. A few days later, Frank got a call from Ed. Unfortunately the cart didn't work as well on the lawn as it had on the blacktop. Frank graciously agreed to take the cart back.

Frank went to Ed's house, loaded the cart, and returned Ed's check. As the two men settled up, Ed, appreciating Frank's accommodating gesture, said, "The Lord's blessing to you." It was a heartfelt exchange between two men who in the past had often talked about balers but rarely exchanged personal expressions of appreciation.

While Frank was loading the cart, one of Ed's fishing buddies, Phares Rutt, stopped by to show Ed his new Roadmaster Buick. After they admired the new Buick and talked about cars for a while, a grandson with Phares asked Ed to autograph his copy of, *The Innovators*, by Homer K. Luttringer. This just-released book told the story of New Holland's dramatic corporate rise after its reorganization under the New Holland men. Ed quickly honored the young boy's request, and signed his book. The delighted grandson enthused, "I just love history!" Showing his quick wit, Ed replied, "Well it's been around a long time!" Frank Weaver also treasures his autographed copy of the book and the memory of Ed's affirming words.[4]

VISITING THE NOLT HOME

Ivan Nolt's family enjoyed visits to the Nolt home. Ivan was Ed's cousin. When Ed left Farmersville, Ivan took over as the local mechanic there. Like Ed, he enjoyed mechanical things more than farming and began repairing cars on his farm. Ivan dismantled Ed's old garage and built a store on the site for his Oliver tractor dealership.

Ed liked Oliver tractors and gave his financial support to Ivan's business. In 1955 he bought the largest tractor Oliver made for his snowplow. Minneapolis-Moline was licensed to manufacture balers with Ed's encouragement. Although Ed received some royalty payments, it was more important for Ed to see his baler associated with his Oliver tractors.[5]

Ivan and Mary Nolt's daughter, Mabel, said it was always interesting to visit the Nolt home. She found it so different from her parents' home. Most unusual, the house included an elevator. While this might have sounded extravagant to people who didn't know the Nolts, it was for Anna's use. She had difficulty climbing stairs due to her health. Ed lamented that her health was one thing money couldn't buy. Mabel remembers that visiting children were allowed one ride up and down on the elevator, no more, but it was a memorable experience.[6]

The Nolts had one of the first dishwashers in their home. Ed bought a microwave oven for his daughter, Vera, from M. S. Sensenig's Store in New Holland. Although Ed was curious about the oven's technology, Vera wasn't impressed with the way it cooked and seldom used it. Their kitchen also had a drinking fountain—a novelty for most homes in those days. Ed had tinkered with the innards of the drinking fountain and added a spigot, making it convenient to fill a water pitcher for use at the table. It was just another example of Ed's fascination with technology, and his penchant for making improvements wherever he saw a need.

A neighborhood friend of the Nolt's son, Eddie, loved going to the Nolt's home to play because he said the toys were more interesting than any of his other friends. Ed motorized a pedal car for the children and equipped it with a device that activated the automatic garage door openers. As the car approached, the door opened and closed again after passing. Then the other door opened for the driver to exit, completing the circuit. However, Eddie's brother, Clarence, drove too fast, the door failed to open in time, and the fun ended with a crash![7]

FAMILY REFLECTIONS

Daughter Vera remembers having fun with her father. He played games such as shuffleboard and darts with the children. Ed also liked to play the accordion and sing. He enjoyed putting cream in his Coke. After meetings with some of the "big guys" at work, Ed would come home and tell Annie all about it. He said their ideas would never work.

Mr. Larry Skromme was Chief Engineer and Head of Engineering during many of Ed's years at New Holland. Frank N. Weaver

Edwin B. Nolt's children: Clarence holding Eddie, and sister Vera. Nolt family photo.

took Ed's grandsons along for a visit with Mr. Skromme in his retirement. During the visit, one of the boys asked, "Were you grandpa's boss?" "Yes," Mr. Skromme replied thoughtfully, "and he never gave me any trouble. He was quiet, cooperative and brilliant!" This was quite a tribute from the chief at New Holland. It was a memorable event for the grandsons, Kenneth, Eugene, Richard and Charlie Burkholder. It so succinctly summed up their grandpa's legacy at New Holland.[8]

In the last year of Ed's life it was time to share his thoughts. Always wary of attention's spotlight, Ed preferred a low profile. He didn't seek recognition, but now he had time to reflect and to talk with those who were close to him.

Near the end of his life, granddaughter Julia Burkholder, sat down with him to record some of his life story. She and her husband, Eugene, lived close to the Nolts and helped out as needed. In their last visit before Ed's passing, he expressed his appreciation for them saying, "You did a lot for me."

While the Nolts wintered in Florida, they took care of the house. In later years, Julia often took Ed for haircuts and waited outside for him in the car. Apparently Ed didn't always carry much cash and likely didn't rely on plastic as many do today. So frequently he came out to the barbershop asking, "Can you pay?" When they ate at one of his favorite restaurants, Julia also ended up paying. By the time they returned home, Ed seemed to have forgotten about these transactions and didn't reimburse his granddaughter. She smiled at the memory. This wasn't Ed, the tightwad, this was grandpa in his advanced years easily distracted.[9]

Ed told Julia that school was boring for him and exams difficult. But he still had a sense of humor about those days. He said that playing ball at noon was his favorite subject. The "school director," as Ed described him, showed less humor as Ed left school for good. He said that Ed would never amount to anything! He compared Ed to his own son, and attributed his son's great success to a proper education.

Although it had happened a long time ago, Ed still remembered the hurtful words, and said he had wanted to prove himself. While this may not have been foremost in his mind during his lifetime, these harsh words did have an effect. Now, near the end of his life, those words resurfaced in his memory. Despite such pronouncements, he could look back and realize what all he had accomplished.

For granddaughter, Julia Burkholder, this time was an opportunity to understand the scope of her grandfather's achievements and the man himself. She wanted a record of Ed's life work. So as she sat with him, he told her about his inventions, and she wrote it all down. As she read the list back to him to make sure she had it right, there were tears in his eyes as he listened to this list of his accomplishments. He also believed in the providential nature of this journey. He shared his conviction that God had shown him how to make his baler in a dream.[10]

During his lifetime, Ed didn't want publicity, yet he appreciated the recognition, especially from ones he loved. This was a safe place for affirmation. When Julia submitted the article about her grandfather to *Farm and Ranch Living*, Ed was interested in the results, and asked occasionally if she had heard from them. For this man who shunned publicity, it seemed that now the time was ripe to publish, to modestly acknowledge in this one-page article, the accomplishments that likely surprised him as much as his skeptical schoolmaster who long ago had written him off in the margins of the uneducated. Unfortunately the article wasn't printed until after Ed's death, but he seemed finally at peace with recognition for what he had done in his lifetime.

Ed helped Julia to understand some of the reasons for his reserved nature. While humility was a deeply held virtue within his faith community, it was also human nature to desire the affirmation and recognition one deserved. Julia had often heard her grandfather caution that once you get to the "top of the ladder," there's only one place to go. This expression echoes the biblical instruction not to be proud of your ability, but to stand firm in the faith because you may fall.

This was the tension he lived with, don't become proud—you're setting yourself up for a fall—but give recognition where deserved.

Much like granddaughter Julia Burkholder's experience, grandson Leon Ray Burkholder found Ed more talkative in his last years. As he was growing up, Leon remembered his grandpa was not one for small talk, but had a quick wit. When someone kidded him that John Eberly actually made the baler, Ed quickly replied that the credit went to a good place! He gave John a lot of credit for what they had accomplished, but let the record speak for itself.

As a child, Leon Ray Burkholder remembered grandfather Ed's bearing as "gruff." Ed's reserved nature and over six feet tall frame could be understandably imposing to a child. Leon remembers him as being more talkative than when he was younger. Leon Ray and his wife, Doris, got to know Ed better while living with him for several months. They were moving in a time of transition. Ed needed someone to stay with him while his second wife, Katie, was hospitalized and later, recuperating at home.

All kidding aside regarding John Eberly's role, Ed told Leon Ray how much he appreciated Eberly and many others who helped him become successful. He especially valued the working relationship he had with George Delp. His brother-in-law, Moses Kurtz's encouragement and financial support were moorings in difficult times. As he had said in an earlier reflection, "Everything just went right."

Even now, Ed was amazed at the timing of events that continued the movement of his baler from his shop in the barn to the global reach of New Holland. It was "luck from one end to another," he told grandson Leon Ray. "It was far from normal." Indeed it was breathtaking to look back at all the fortunate moments, the meetings of men who gave space for Ed's inventive mind to create while they provided concrete means for that expression to grow.[11]

One might be surprised to hear Ed refer to "everything just going right" as simply good luck. When talking with granddaughter,

Julia, Ed shared his belief that God had shown him how to make the baler. Some believe the English term, luck, doesn't adequately express the sentiment of the Pennsylvania Dutch term, *glick*, or luck. For them, *glick* is more than random good fortune. In a fortunate chain of events, they would suggest that God has been at work in some way, rather than the events being purely luck. While we don't know what was in Ed's mind, it seems likely that, for him, luck and divine intervention weren't mutually exclusive.

To borrow an analogy from the world of sport, it has been said that sometimes an athlete has to be good in order to be lucky. The fortuitous bounce of a golf ball onto the green instead of into the unplayable lie of a hazard could be attributed to luck, but the persistent, grinding play of a skilled golfer, might earn him a victory in the winner's circle. He or she may have had some luck along the way, but they were also very good.

For Ed Nolt and the New Holland men on this journey, there were some lucky "bounces" along the way, but these were also men with great abilities who were willing to play the risk-reward game of entrepreneurship. They brought a significant array of talents to the table and the willingness to test them. There was reason to stand back and be amazed—lucky, yes but they were also very good!

IN TRIBUTE

How does one end Ed Nolt's story? Ironically, perhaps with unsolicited tributes—the very thing Ed shunned. There is a need for conscious acknowledgement of his life and legacy. These tributes give authentic recognition of a unique and gifted man, made all the more genuine by his reluctance to seek such accolades.

After Ed Nolt's passing in 1992, Ivan Glick wrote a tribute to him in the *Lancaster Farming Magazine*. Glick noted that a stranger would never have guessed the genius of this quiet, reserved man. Not many people who worked at New Holland knew Ed well, or that his invention was the foundation for New Holland's early success in the

1940's. Ed wanted it that way. Perhaps Glick most eloquently gave voice to Ed Nolt's philosophy of life in words even Ed couldn't speak but lived:

> In his view, as a Christian, it would have been just plain wrong to accept fame or to have people know about his charity. Brotherhood and Christian fellowship were more important to him. Being a stand-out would have interfered with things he believed…his parents taught him to be humble and the importance of Christian stewardship.[12]

While such a tribute might have embarrassed Ed, he would have resonated with its spirit.

Joseph A. Brown wrote a letter of tribute to the *Lancaster New Era* soon after Ed's passing. He was familiar with Ed's work as New Holland's patent attorney. He believed Ed was fortunate to have New Holland recognize him for the "rare gem" he was—this man with little formal education and no engineering degree. "They gave him the opportunity to do his thing." In a printed statement of recognition by the United States Patent Office, Ed requested that his name not be used. "It merely referred to him as a Lancaster County farmer."

Brown concluded his letter maintaining that Ed Nolt belonged on a list of the top 100 inventors of the past 50 years as a remarkable man—"Lancaster County, the United States and the world were blessed by his presence."[13]

SUMMATION

One could imagine Ed Nolt looking up from his New Holland workbench, and gazing out upon a procession of departing, baler-laden railroad cars. Was this too, only a dream? He remembered wrestling with the problems of his first baler in that winter shop so long ago. In that dream, his work was so vivid he expected the finished piece to be on his workbench the next morning. Although it wasn't there, he contin-

100th Annual EMI Convention

September 25-27, 1993 • Fairmont Hotel • Chicago, Illinois

100 MOST SIGNIFICANT CONTRIBUTOR

On the occasion of the 100th Convention of the Equipment Manufacturers Institute, the EMI Board of Directors honored a select group of individuals whose contributions to the mechanization of agriculture and construction during the Institute's first one hundred years (1893-1993) was so significant as to merit special industry recognition.

EDWIN B. NOLT

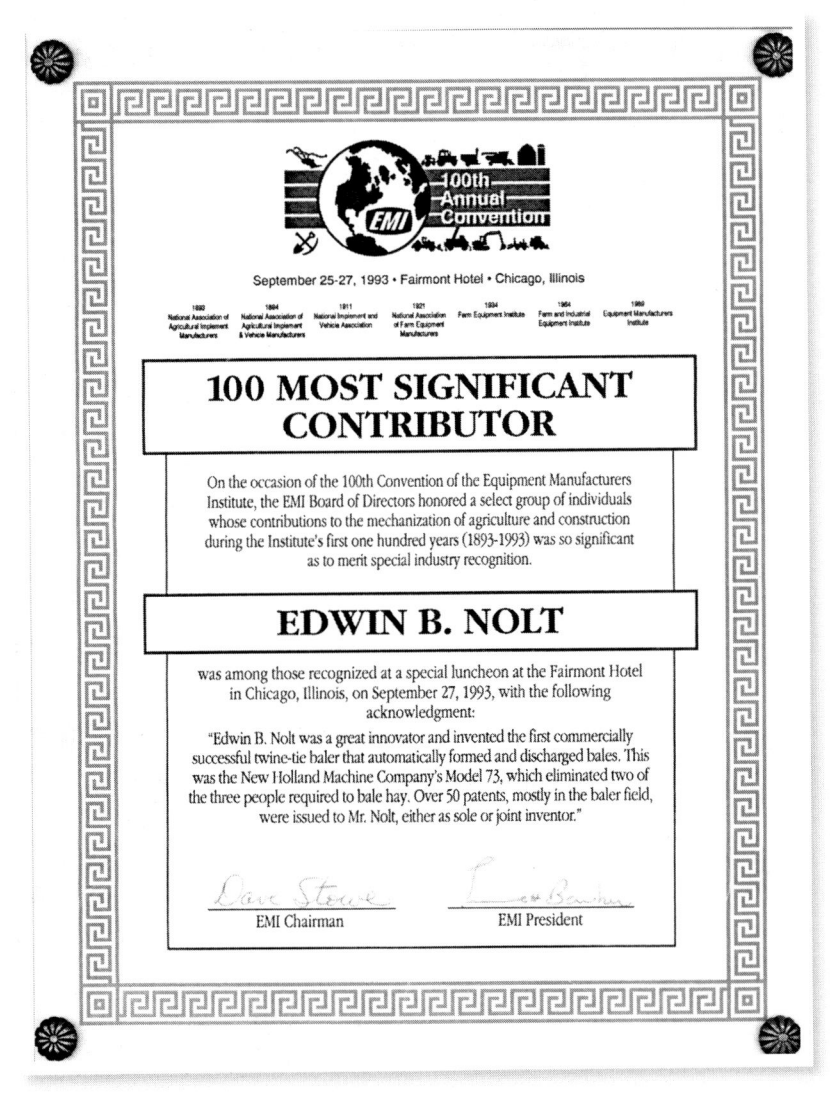

was among those recognized at a special luncheon at the Fairmont Hotel in Chicago, Illinois, on September 27, 1993, with the following acknowledgment:

"Edwin B. Nolt was a great innovator and invented the first commercially successful twine-tie baler that automatically formed and discharged bales. This was the New Holland Machine Company's Model 73, which eliminated two of the three people required to bale hay. Over 50 patents, mostly in the baler field, were issued to Mr. Nolt, either as sole or joint inventor."

EMI Chairman   EMI President

A plaque given posthumously to Edwin B. Nolt for being one of the 100 Most Significant Contributors to the farm machinery industry. NHAHS Collection.

ued working on his dream. But now, this was not a dream; it was reality, though sometimes just as hard to believe. Through hard work and the perseverance of a brilliant mind, things had indeed gone just right.

It's ironic that Ed Nolt, who never enjoyed farming, referred to himself, and preferred to be known, as just a simple farmer. I believe this image speaks of the deeply held values and identity that even Ed Nolt would have had difficulty expressing. Late in his life, as he listened to granddaughter Julia Burkholder recite his life accomplishments, the tears came. His emotions reflected an emotional and spiritual journey of memories at the core of his being.

Throughout life, his Mennonite faith, family and cultural values anchored him. He remained grounded in this identity. Wealth did change Ed Nolt to a degree as he enjoyed a lifestyle not typical of his people. Like many of other faiths, Ed lived within those boundaries in some areas while stretching beyond them in others. He remembered the deeply ingrained life lessons he had learned in his past: beware of pride and self-promotion; with money comes responsibility and unwanted attention; hard work and success should be rewarded.

The farm symbolized this past identity as he stepped into a bewilderingly different world beginning with an educational system that failed to nurture his creative genius, and worse, left him with a negative self-image. For some, memory of Ed's educational shortcomings still remain when they speak of him today. The schoolmaster's assessment that Ed Nolt wouldn't amount to anything due to his lack of education festered in his memory. He left school for the farm and found his craft there in the medium of metal and machinery. Here, despite the skepticism of some, his brilliance would blossom through an intensity and perseverance incomprehensible to the fainthearted.

His journey into the corporate world began as he left Farmersville. Refinements of his baler at Kinzers brought with it the new opportunities and challenges of mass production, finances and marketing. This was the vestibule to the corporate world Ed entered at New Holland. Aside from the sheer genius and grit of Ed Nolt, perhaps the most amazing part of this story was that at every critical juncture, Ed found the people and resources—or they found him—needed to reach the next level of his journey. The New Holland men played a huge role in the corporate phase by giving him space—"Ed's Room in Experimental"—where he continued to use his gifts. Ed's room was his sanctuary; it was the place where he was most comfortable expressing through metal what was in his mind. Ed Nolt built the baler that was New Holland's lifeline to corporate success in its early years. New Holland recognized his genius and the mutual benefits of their relationship.

Geroge Delp's advice and friendship were extremely helpful to Ed in navigating this corporate world. Through the years at New Holland, he protected Ed's room from the encroachments of others. He honored the financial obligations the company made to Ed and went beyond them. He helped Ed avoid the financial maze of success that allowed him to concentrate on what he loved most, tinkering in his shop.

Ed's friendship with Shaun Seymour enabled him to bridge the gap between the blacksmith engineers and the professionals, but it was more than that. These two men from very different backgrounds and experiences were simply friends. As innovators, they learned from each other, and were comfortable with each other. They understood the peculiarities of inventors.

On occasion, as Ed and other engineers field-tested new equipment, he would slip away, returning with a trunk full of treats for a break in their long hours. Among other goodies, there would be sodas and Milky Way candy bars. Shaun Seymour remembers that if there were just a few men, Ed might remain on the edges of the conversations around the refreshments, but if the group were larger, he would soon wander off to himself, seeking some solitude, and perhaps space to ponder a solution to their problem.

But more than this, Ed retreated from such groups out of fear that if he joined in the engineers' conversation, they would think he was "dumb." He expressed this sentiment to Seymour on more than one occasion. It was likely one of the reasons he was a man of few words. Cautious of others' appraisal, he was careful to guard his words.

When Ed Nolt left Farmersville, he took with him life lessons and the identity of the farm, the positives and negatives of his past, and his God-given abilities. As we attempt to understand who Ed Nolt was, it is important to understand and appreciate the many components that shaped his life, to marvel and accept him for the unique person he was, and for what he accomplished.

He manifested many qualities of the introvert. He was careful to keep his thoughts and emotions to himself. His quiet reserve made it difficult to get to know him. He was uncomfortable in social situations. He was most relaxed in small groups of close friends. He was inquisitive and enjoyed understanding details of how things worked. He studied things carefully before voicing his ideas. Although there are many aspects of his life to consider in attempting to understand Ed Nolt, his personality gives us some insights. It's just who he was, Ed!

APPENDIX: *1964 Interview*

The following pages are an excerpt of the author's 1964 interview and college history seminar paper on the history of The New Holland Machine Company. Ed Nolt granted the interview with the agreement that his name would not be used, and it was only accessible to professor, Dr. John A. Lapp. To honor this request, Ed Nolt became the "local farmer" of this New Holland story. The complete paper is available at the New Holland Area Historical Society museum.

A HISTORY OF NEW HOLLAND MACHINE COMPANY

For: History Seminar (History 408)
    Mr. John A. Lapp

Submitted by:
    Allan W. Shirk
    Eastern Mennonite College
    May 26, 1965

III. THE REVOLUTIONIZATION OF GRASSLAND FARMING

The story of New Holland Machine Company would not be complete without continuing with the development of the automatic baler. Without this new product, it would likely have been difficult to regain the earlier prosperity the company once enjoyed.

The field pickup baler which was brought out in 1932 ultimately led to the next step of development. This was the development of the automatic baler. Although the pickup baler took the hay directly from the window, two or three men were needed to tie the bales and operate the baler. With the automatic baler, only one man is needed to drive the tractor. The baler picks up the hay; it is compressed into a bale which is tied by a mechanical knotter. The bales pass through the baler and are dropped behind as it moves on.

The invention of the automatic baler began when a Lancaster County farmer became interested in purchasing a baler. The farmer did custom threshing, and he wanted a baler to bale the loose straw. He saw an advertisement in the *Farm Journal* which featured a lightweight baler. The baler packed the bales with an augerlike feeding action and tied the bales with twine. Deciding that this baler would suit his purposes, he purchased one from a midwestern company.

When the farmer tried his new baler in the field, it created only a tangled mess of twine and straw. After this, he tried a Case baler. It was too heavy and took four men to operate, since it didn't have a knotter.

In the fall of 1936, the farmer took his baler apart in a barn behind his home. He also operated a service station at his home in Farmersville, Pennsylvania. He used the knotter, as well as the idea of stopping the plunger, from the baler he had bought in making his own baler.

The farmer had discovered what was causing the trouble in the baler he had bought. The continuous strokes of the plunger which packed hay into the bale chamber interfered with the tying process. To solve this, he made an eccentric cam. The cam inactivated the plunger action for a full stroke during which the bale was tied.

In the spring of 1937, the first automatic baler emerged from the farmer's barn. It was a mixture of parts from a wood saw, a grain combine, a tractor, an automobile, and other parts such as the cam which the inventor made himself. It might have been considered a creation of modern art by someone from the city.

Improvements were made on the baler during the summer. The inventor did custom baling to see how well his baler would perform. Several improvements had to be made. The baler had a standard grain combine pickup. The pickup cylinder wrapped badly at times. There was also the problem of how to get uniform pickup from the windrow and, in cross feeding, from the pickup to the bale chamber. There was also trouble in getting the material under the wadboard (the flat part of the plunger which packed the material) so it could be compressed by the plunger. The knotter did not function well at times.

At the end of the 1937 season, the farmer was discouraged and decided to abandon his project. If it had not been for the persuasion of some friends, he might have decided to forget the whole project. He was encouraged, however, and made another attempt to get the "bugs" out of his machine.

In the winter of 1938, he built five balers by hand at Arthur Young's machine shop in Kinzers, Pennsylvania. It was on these balers that the plunger was halted by the eccentric cam during the tying cycle. This enabled the material to be held under compression while it was being tied. The wadboard action was changed. The plunger pushed the material in slowly and retreated quickly. This solved the earlier wadboard problem. A knife was attached to the plunger. The knife made neat bale sections with no material overlapping between bales. This made the separation of the bales much easier.

These five balers were used in custom baling during the summer of 1938. Minor improvements were made as needed. A heavier knotter had been made by the inventor and was used on all the balers produced after his first attempt. In 1939, thirty more balers were built at Young's and ninety in 1940. In the fall of 1940, production shifted to the New Holland Machine Company which had been organized that year. Here the baler was put into mass production.

This is the story of the first automatic baler. Some of the problems which confronted the inventor have been related. Perhaps some of the discouragements and frustrations which all inventors likely face have not been told. The new baler was a tribute to the mechanical skill of its builder. His ability to see where others had made mistakes helped him to succeed which they had failed.

The automatic baler was the first of a series of products, offered by New Holland, which have made haymaking a one-man system. The hay-in-a-day system offered by New Holland enables a farmer to harvest his hay crop single-handedly. With New Holland's combination mower and hay conditioner, the farmer can do two jobs in one. This also reduces field drying time by thirty to fifty per cent. Raking at the proper time prevents shattering of the leaves; this insures higher protein content and better hay.

The bale thrower developed by New Holland has also proven to be a labor-saving device. It does the work of two men. The loading capacity of a wagon with six foot sides loaded by a bale thrower is about the same as a wagon hand loaded and having five foot sides.

Another option to the bale thrower is the New Holland stackcruiser. This is a motorized wagon which the farmer can use to pick up bales from the ground. The stackcruiser also stacks the bales without their being touched by the farmer. A stack retriever is also available to farmers. With this device mounted on a dump truck, the farmer can relocate a stackcruiser load in one operation.

New Holland crop dryers can be used to dry hay while still on the wagons or in a shed. Dryers have been used less since the introduction of hay crushers which allow the hay to dry more quickly in the field.

Endnotes

CHAPTER 1: THE FORMATIVE YEARS

1. "An Interview with Ed Nolt." Swiss Pioneer Preservation Associates. 1986-1988, CD. Ivan Glick passed on tapes of an interview done in the latter years of Ed Nolt's life. The Associates transferred the tapes to a CD. The date is approximate and the interviewer is unknown.

2. Weaver, Frank N. Personal interview, 29 Nov. 2014.

3. R. Wesley Newswanger, *The Professional Life of A Lancaster County, Pennsylvania, Inventor* (Millersville University, 1984), 2.

4. "Family Stories About Ed Nolt," 20 Jun. 2013.

5. Homer K. Luttringer, *The Innovators: The New Holland Story* (Lancaster, PA: Homer K. Luttringer, 1990), 26.

6. Seymour, Shaun. Personal interview, 17 Feb. 2015.

7. Weaver, Frank N.; Seymour, Shaun. Personal interview, 3 Oct. 2014.

8. Luttringer, 26-27.

9. "An Interview with Ed Nolt." CD.

10. Luttringer, 26-27.

11. *The Ephrata Review.* 13 Jan. 1928.

12. *The Ephrata Review.* 10 Feb. 1933; Weaver, Luke. Personal interview, 28 Jan. 2015.

13. Gehman, David. Personal interview, 17 Apr. 2014.

14. "Family Stories About Ed Nolt," 20 Jun. 2013.

15. Luttringer, 27.

16. Burkholder, Leon Ray. Phone interview, 23 Mar. 2015.

17. "An Interview with Ed Nolt." CD.

18. Martin, Henry; Weaver, Luke. Personal interview, 18 Feb. 2015.

19. Burkholder, Leon Ray. Personal interview, 23 Mar. 2015.

20. Martin, Henry. Personal interview, 18 Feb. 2015.

21. Weaver, Frank N. Personal interview, 29 Nov. 2014. Unlike his other factual stories included in this book, this one imagines "little Eddie's" inventive nature as a boy. The V-plow story is factual.

22. Zimmerman, Raymond. Personal interview, 8 May 2015.

23. Seymour, Shaun. Personal interview, 21 Nov. 2014.

24. Newswanger, 3.

25. Seymour, Shaun. Personal interview, 21 Nov. 2014.

CHAPTER 2: WORKING ON THE NOLT SPECIAL

1. Seymour, Shaun. Personal interview, 26 Feb. 2015.

2. "Family Meeting: Stories About Ed Nolt," 20 Jun. 2013.

3. Ibid.

4. United States Patent Office approval no. 2,236,628, "Means for Bailing Material," Edwin B. Nolt, Farmersville, Pa. Application, 9 Apr. 1938, Serial No. 201,089. 1 Apr. 1941, declaration, 6.

5. "An Interview with Ed Nolt." CD.

6. Weaver, Frank N. Personal interview, 29 Nov. 2014.

7. "New Holland, Our First 100 Years, 1895-1995," (Communication and Sales Department) 12.

8. "The Story of the Baler," *The New Holland Line*, Mar. 1946, 5.

9. Luttringer, 27.

10. "William Chester Ruth," In *Encyclopedia of Significant People and Places in African American History Online*. Retrieved from http://www.blackpast.org/aah/ruth-william-chester-1882-1971.

11. "An Interview with Ed Nolt." CD.

12. Glick, 11.

13. Burkholder, Leon Ray. Phone interview, 23 Mar. 2015.

14. Martin, Henry. Personal interview, 18 Feb. 2015.

15. Delp, George C. to Edwin B. Nolt, 17 Apr. 1956.

CHAPTER 3: MOVING BEYOND FARMERSVILLE

1. Glick, 11.
2. Seymour, Shaun. Personal interview, 26 Feb. 2015.
3. Ibid.
4. Burkholder, Leon Ray. Phone interview, 23 Mar. 2015.
5. Seymour, Shaun. Personal interview, 26 Feb. 2015.
6. Tallman, Robert. "Bob's Tales," unpublished.? 20.
7. "An Interview with Ed Nolt." CD.
8. Ibid.
9. Seymour, Shaun. Personal interview, 26 Feb. 2015.
10. "An Interview with Ed Nolt." CD.
11. Glick, 11-12.
12. Luttringer, 29.
13. Shirk, Allan W., *A History of New Holland Machine Company* (The Pennsylvania State University, 1965), 11.
14. Ibid., 13.
15. Ibid., 8, 10-11.
16. Ibid., 12.
17. Glick, 12.
18. Burkholder, Leon Ray. Phone interview, 23 Mar. 2015.
19. "Family Breakfast Stories," 13 Mar. 2015.
20. "An Interview with Ed Nolt." CD.
21. Glick, 13.
22. "An Interview with Ed Nolt." CD.
23. Seymour, Shaun. Personal interview, 26 Feb. 2015.; Seymour, Shaun. "Henry Fisher." Message to Don Horning, 16 Feb. 2015. E-mail.
24. Luttringer, 26.
25. Seymour, Shaun, Personal interview, 7 Nov. 2014.

CHAPTER 4: THE NEW HOLLAND BONANZA

1. Frankhouser, Brian, "Description of New Holland in the 1940's." Message to Allan W. Shirk, 15 Apr. 2015. E-mail. Grandson

Galen Rutt still treasures silver dollars given to him by his grandfather, Mahlon Rutt. Mahlon worked in the Press and Shear department for 15 years.

2. Seymour, Shaun. Personal interview, 15 Sep. 2014.

3. "An Interview with Ed Nolt." CD.

4. Shirk, 15-16.

5. Ibid., 16.

6. Seymour, Shaun; Weaver, Frank N. Personal interview, 3 Oct. 2014.

7. Nelson, Clarence J. to Kenneth Burkholder, 23 Sep. 1995.

8. Hoover, Amos B., "Language Struggles Among Old Order Mennonites in Lancaster County," *Muddy Creek Review*, Vol. 3 (2012), 6.

9. Hoover, Amos B., "German Language: Cradle of Our Heritage" (unpublished).

10. Hoover, Amos B. Personal interview, 21 May 2015.

11. Ira D. Landis and Richard D. Thiessen, "Weaverland Mennonite Conference." *Global Anabaptist Mennonite Encyclopedia Online*. October 2010. Web. 10 May 2015.

12. Seymour, Shaun. Personal interview, 19 Dec. 2014.

13. Glick, 15.

14. Seymour, Shaun. Personal interview, 21 Nov. 2014.

15. Glick, 14-16; "It's the New Model 66!," *The New Holland Line*, Dec. 1952, 5-6.

16. Weaver, Frank N.; Seymour, Shaun. Personal interview, 29 Nov. 2014; 19 Dec. 2014.

17. Seymour, Shaun. Personal interview, 19 Dec. 2014. Weaver, Frank N. "Notes and Reflections on the Model 166," 2014.

18. Peters, L. E. to Allan W. Shirk, 10 May 1965.

19. Glick, 75-76.

20. "From Balers to Fish Chummers: FBH Patents Run Gamut." *The Reporter*, May 1994, 4.

21. Joseph A. Brown, "Baler Inventor A Remarkable Man." *Lancaster New Era*, 8 May 1992.

CHAPTER 5: "IT CHANGED EVERYTHING"

1. Beam, Richard, *The Ephrata Review*, 4 Mar. 1981.
2. Delp, George C. to Edwin B. Nolt, 17 Apr. 1956. 2.
3. Ibid., 8.
4. Ibid., 8.
5. Delp, George C. to Edwin B. Nolt, 17 Jan 1949.
6. Burkholder, Kenneth. Personal interview, 13 Mar. 2015.
7. Weaver, Frank N. Personal interview, 8 Aug. 2014.
8. Wissler, Robert U. "The Ephrata Community Hospital: From its Founding to 1961." *Journal of the Historical Society of the Cocalico Valley Volume XII. (1987): 11-15.*
9. Weaver, Frank N.; Nolt Hurst, Mabel. Personal interview, 14 Oct. 2014.
10. Ibid.
11. Weaver, Frank N. Personal interview, 29 Nov. 2014.
12. Clarence J. Nelson to Kenneth Burkholder, 23 Sep. 1955, 2.
13. Ibid., 2.
14. Ibid., 5.
15. Public Domain IRS 990pf.
16. Clarence J. Nelson to Kenneth Burkholder, 23 Sep. 1995.
17. Glick, 77.

CHAPTER 6: THE LATER YEARS

1. Horning, Don. Message to Allan W. Shirk, 24 May 2015. Email. Jeff Shirk was a New Holland employee who related this story.
2. Weaver, Frank N. Personal interview, 7 Nov. 2014.
3. Weaver, Frank N. Personal interview, 3 Oct. 2014.
4. Weaver, Frank N. Personal interview, 29 Nov. 2014.
5. Burkholder, Kenneth. Personal interview, 31 Mar. 2015. In the letter, Mr. Delp indicates Minneapolis-Moline Power Implement Company manufactured 2,032 balers between November 1, 1947,

and October 31, 1948, for which Ed Nolt received a royalty of $12.50 per baler.

    6. Nolt Hurst, Mabel. Personal interview, 24 Oct. 2014.

    7. "Family Breakfast Stories," 13 Mar. 2015.

    8. Weaver, Frank N. "Notes of Visit to Larry Skromme," 16 Nov. 2010.

    9. Burkholder, Julia. Personal interview, 4 Mar. 2015.

    10. Burkholder, Julia, "God Helped Grandpa Build a Better Baler," *Farm and Ranch Living*, Apr.-May 1993, 38.

    11. Burkholder, Leon Ray. Phone interview, 23 Mar. 2015.

    12. Glick, Ivan, "Inventor of Baler Dies But Contribution to Farming Lives Forever," *Lancaster Farming*, Vol. 37, No. 24, Saturday, Apr. 25, 1992, 1, 24.

    13. Brown, Joseph A., "Baler Inventor A Remarkable Man," *Lancaster New Era*, 5/8/1992.

Works Cited

"An Interview with Ed Nolt." *Swiss Pioneer Preservation Associates,* 1986-1988, CD.

Brown, Joseph A. Letter to editor. "Baler Inventor a Remarkable Man." *Lancaster New Era,* 8 May 1992. Print.

Burkholder, Julia. "God Helped Grandpa Build a Better Baler." *Farm and Ranch Living,* Apr.-May 1993, p. 38. Print.

Burkholder, Kenneth. "CRELS Grants." Message to Don Horning, 16 Mar. 2015. Email.

Delp, George C. to Edwin B. Nolt, 17 Jan. 1949. Print.

Glick, Ivan. *Mr. Fisher's Company: History of New Holland 1940-1985.* Martindale, PA: The Swiss Pioneer Preservation Associates, 2007. Print.

——— "Inventor of Baler Dies But Contribution to Farming Lives Forever." *Lancaster Farming,* 25 Apr. 1992, 1, 24. Print.

"Family Breakfast Stories," 13 Mar. 2015.

"Family Meeting: Stories About Ed Nolt," 20 Jun. 2013.

Frankhouser, Brian. "Re: Description of New Holland in the 1940's." Message to Allan W. Shirk, 15 Apr. 2015. E-mail.

"From Balers to Fish Chummers: FNH Patents Run Gamut." *The Reporter,* May 1994, p. 4. Print.

Global Anabaptist Encyclopedia Online, "Weaverland Mennonite Conference," 27 Jul. 2014.

Hoover, Amos B. "Language Struggles Among Old Order Mennonites in Lancaster County." *Muddy Creek Review,* Vol. 3, 2012, pp. 5-9. Print.

———— *German Language: Cradle of Our Heritage.* Unpublished.
Horning, Don. Message to Allan W. Shirk, 24 May 2015. Email.
"It's the New Model 66!," *The New Holland Line*, Dec. 1952, pp. 5-6. Print.
Landis, Ira D. and Richard D. Thiessen. "Weaverland Mennonite Conference." *Global Anabaptist Mennonite Encyclopedia Online.* October 2010. Web. 10 May 2015.
Luttringer, Homer K. *The Innovators: The New Holland Story.* Lancaster, PA: Homer K. Luttringer, 1990. Print.
Nelson, Clarence J. to Kenneth Burkholder, 23 Sep. 1995. Print.
New Holland, Our First 100 Years, 1895-1995. (Communication and Sales Department) p. 12. Print.
Newswanger, R. Wesley. "The Professional Life of a Lancaster County, Pennsylvania, Inventor." Millersville University, 1984. Print
Peters, L. E. to Allan W. Shirk, 10 May 1965. Print.
Seymour, Shaun. Message to Don Horning, 16 Feb. 2015. E-mail.
Shirk, Allan W. "A History of New Holland Machine Company." Eastern Mennonite College, 1965. Print.
Tallman, Robert. "Bob's Tales." Unpublished.
The Ephrata Review. 13 Jan. 1928; 10 Feb. 1933; 4 Mar. 1981. Print.
"The Story of the Baler...Earl Township Thresherman, Inventor of New Holland Automaton Hay Press, Builds First Machine in Temporary Workshop Set Up in His Barn." Mar. 1948. *The New Holland Line,* Mar. 1946, 5-6. Print.
United States Patent Office approval no. 2,236,628, 1 Apr. 1941. "Means for Bailing Material," Edwin B. Nolt, Farmersville, Pa. Application, 9 Apr. 1938, Serial No. 201,089. Print.
Weaver, Frank N. "Notes of Visit to Mr. Larry Skromme." 16 Nov. 2010. Print.
"William Chester Ruth," *Online Encyclopedia of Significant People and Places in African American History.*
Wissler, Robert U. "The Ephrata Community Hospital: From its Founding to 1961." *Journal of the Historical Society of the Cocalico Valley Volume XII. (1987): 11-15.* Print.

"1937, The New Holland Baler." *New Holland, Our First 100 Years,1895-1995.* New Holland: Communication and Sales Department, 1995. Print.

INTERVIEWS BY AUTHOR
    Burkholder, Julia. 5 Sep. 2014; 14 Mar. 2015.
    Burkholder, Kenneth. 2014-2015.
    Burkholder, Leon Ray. Phone interview, 23 Mar. 2015.
    Gehman, David. 17 Apr. 2014.
    Hoover, Amos B. 1 Apr. 2015; 21 May 2015; 27 May 2015.
    Hurst, Mabel Nolt. 24 Oct 2014.
    Martin, Henry. 18 Feb. 2015.
    Seymour, Shaun. 2013-2015.
    Weaver, Frank N. 2014-2015.
    Weaver, Luke. 31 Jan. 2014; 28 Jan. 2015; 18 Feb. 2015; 3 May 2015.
    Zimmerman, Raymond. 8 May 2015.

Other Stories

Many stories have been told about Ed Nolt. Some are well documented, others are passed on as truth. While some cannot be authenticated, they often contain an element of truth. Upon hearing the following story, a grandson replied that it sounded like grandpa. That is the spirit in which these stories are related.

HELPING A FARMER

Perhaps the story heard most frequently, though details vary, is the following: When Ed was traveling he always carried tools in the car. On a trip with his fishing buddies, he saw a farmer in a field working on a New Holland baler. Ed stopped and talked with the farmer about his problem and then said he believed he could help. He got his tools and fixed the baler. "Go ahead, it will work now," Ed said, and it did. He left without telling the farmer who he was. A neighbor saw the whole thing and asked the farmer the next day if he knew who had fixed his baler. The farmer didn't know who it was. When told it was Ed Nolt, the inventor of the New Holland baler, the farmer refused to believe this ordinary looking man's true identity.

FRUGALITY

Ed was traveling by car with a friend. As they approached a service station, the driver prepared to stop for gas. Ed encouraged him to go on a just few more miles where he knew the gas was a few cents cheaper.

In the 1980's, several people from each plant were planning to attend a company meeting in Grand Island, Nebraska. Ed Nolt sat down and figured out it would be cheaper to fly and save on motel bills. He called Philadelphia Airport and chartered a jet for the company. Someone said if Bob Ressler hears about this he won't be at all happy!

HUMOR

Ed was having fun with a neighborhood family regarding their car full of children. He told the neighbor his car looked like a jar of pickles going down the road with everyone packed in. The neighbor said that at least his car didn't rattle. Ed replied that it was the money in his car that rattled!

A WILD RIDE

Brother Joe loved his horses. He wanted the best and fastest horse in the neighborhood. On one occasion Joe spotted a town rival just ahead. Building up a head of steam on his unsuspecting quarry, Joe blew by him with a pleased goodbye wave.

Another horse episode, however, could have bruised more than egos. Ed's father was riding with his two sons up *Katz Boucle Weeg* (Cat's Back Road) on Joe's wagon where Fairmount Homes is located today. As they climbed to the crest of the ridge, Ed's father asked Joe, *"Kenna diese gile net springa?"* (Can't these horses run?) That was the wrong thing to say to Joe, who with the crack of his whip, spurred his team on to a wild ride careening downhill on this crooked, winding road. They held on for dear life. Fortunately all survived, newly impressed with Joe's horses.

A MISSED OPPORTUNITY?

The following story is one reason some think Joe was one of Ed's backers. Joe, prone to embellishment, related this story to a friend. He had strong doubts in the early stages of the project. At some point in the new venture, according to Joe, Ed offered him a partnership in the business. Joe declined for reasons that aren't clear. He did enjoy driving his truck and hauling farm-related freight. Later he found farming more to his liking than Ed had, and became a successful farmer. Reflecting on Ed's long-past offer, Joe told a neighbor living on the former Nolt farm, "That was a dumb idea"—not accepting Ed's proposal. "But," he summed up, "I have a lot of money. Ed just has more!" It was vintage, easy-going *"drie steochig"* (three-story) Joe. He didn't brood on this lost opportunity. He had found his own way to be successful.

SUNDAY CIGARS

Sunday dinners ended with cigars for the men. Ed liked to smoke and handed out the cigars as did other hosts when the family was at their homes. The living room usually became blue with smoke. Finally one aunt said, "No more smoking in my house!" The men then retired to the tobacco stripping room for their cigars. The nephew concluded the story by saying that his dad never smoked because of health concerns, but they raised over 20 acres of tobacco.

AIR CONDITIONING

Air conditioning was becoming available in cars but was still seen as a luxury. Ed was asked why he didn't have air conditioning in his car since he could obviously afford it. He replied, "I'll have air conditioning when you can put in the seat where I need it!"

DON'T COUNT YOUR CHICKENS...

While planning to build a chicken house, a nephew said, "I'll ask my rich uncle for the money." His father went along to see Ed, but may not have gone inside with him. When the nephew made his request, Ed responded that if he begins giving money to nephews, where will it end! He never got the money and said perhaps it was best. He thinks his father may have given Ed some inkling of the coming visit and request.

STRONG HANDS

While field testing a baler with Ed, Randy Sierk said they needed to replace a rod on the baler. Ed began to tighten the nuts with his hands. Randy volunteered to get Ed a wrench. Ed replied in his familiar deep voice, "I don't need no wrench!" He continued to tighten the nuts with his big hands.

Later when Randy tried to use a wrench to tighten the nuts, he realized Ed didn't need any assistance.

NOT A UNION MAN

Wilbur Horning remembers Bob Ressler speaking at a Garden Spot school assembly. As a student, Wilbur felt respect for Mr. Ressler. He remembers that Ressler was very much against unions and said there is no place for a union in your company if you treated the employees right. New Holland did live up to this challenge. Several union votes failed. One year a prospective engineer was hired as a summer intern at New Holland. When it was learned that his mother was a union steward, this apparently affected the young man's standing. He lasted three days and then was gone!

SEEKING ADVICE

Another local inventor, Luke Wenger, remembers as a young boy when the New Holland test crew would come to bale hay on his family's Leola farm. The machinery was covered with tarps and a well-dressed man—possibly an engineer—appeared to "stand guard" close by the machinery trailer. "We kept our distance," Luke said. "We knew we were not welcome to inspect things close up, but we got our hay baled."

Years later, Luke visited Ed Nolt in his own kitchen to get some advice. Working in his garage, Luke had perfected a device to measure oxygen flow. Hospitals were interested and ready to purchase the product. Luke's father questioned the wisdom of his son's plan to manufacture the instrument himself. He suggested they talk to Ed. While Ed didn't express a strong opinion, he might have been a factor in Luke's decision. His Time Meter company began to manufacture the device at his own local plant.

TWO BROTHERS: A CONTRAST OF PERSONALITIES

Joe hauled 25-pound sacks of potatoes to Philadelphia for Henry Hoover. When he stopped at traffic lights in Philly, sometimes boys crawled on the truck and threw off potato bags to their accomplices. So he kept watching for such action. On the way home with his empty truck, he saw a boy climb aboard. Due to the truck's high sides, the youth couldn't see the truck didn't have any plunder, so he attempted to disembark. Seeing this, Joe hit the brakes and the boy slid to the front of the bed. Joe timed the traffic lights so that he didn't have to stop, keeping the boy captive. The kid was hollering to let him off, but Joe just kept going a long way from that neighborhood before finally letting him off the truck. Joe said he didn't care if the boy "hollered," he just wanted to teach him a lesson.

Joe didn't tell the stories where he didn't fare as well but he must have told someone this one. One day on his Philadelphia trip, some boys stole his canvas tarp from the truck. Apparently this was a big concern. Joe needed a tarp so later that day he bought one from some boys on the street. When he got home, he realized he had bought back his own tarp!

One day Joe was driving his truck down a hill. In the distance, a Model A Ford entered the road, preparing to turn left to go uphill, but the car stalled in the middle of the road. Bearing down on the stalled car, Joe started blowing his horn, and watched as the poor driver worked frantically to restart his car. When the driver got the car going again, he floored it, escaping into a field directly across the road to avoid disaster. Joe could have stopped if necessary but he wanted to have some fun—at someone else's expense!

People walking or riding past the Nolt home in Farmersville were often in conversation with Joe as they passed by. Conversations would be shouted to each other as they moved on. Ed was not one to engage in this kind of interchange but Joe could be counted on to address anyone he saw passing by. One day he was struggling with a bucking rototiller tractor in the garden. Looking up, he yelled at the passerby, "Don't you laugh!" He never missed an opportunity for social engagement.

Joe was always ready for a little mischief, or *"dumbheit."* While working at Ressler's Cabinetry shop, one of his jobs was to glue chair spindles into place. Whenever a well-dressed salesman was close by, Joe added extra glue to the job and timed his hammering of the spindles to "accidentally" spray the excess glue on his unaware victim.

On another occasion, Joe tampered with a tractor magneto and then arrived late for work with Ed and the crew the next morning. Nobody could work until the tractor was fixed so Joe, pretending to assess the situation, soon discovered the problem and "fixed" the tractor, demonstrating his superior talents to all.

Long-time Farmersville resident, Henry Martin summed up these stories about the two brothers by saying, "You didn't hear stories like that from Ed. He was totally different."

BOYS WILL BE BOYS

As boys, Ed would take things apart to see how they worked. On the other hand, Joe ran things until they flew apart! In his little shop his father made for fixing farm equipment Ed did things that his dad didn't know about. One day Ed decided to fill a 50-gallon barrel with air to see how much it would take to make it explode. Fortunately someone, perhaps his mother, stopped him before the explosion.

JOE BECOMES A BELIEVER

When Ed moved his baler to Art Young's it wasn't perfect, it needed refinement but it was working. Ed tried it out on cousin Henry Hoover's farm after combining Henry's crop, he used his baler for the straw. Neighbors came out to watch this new contraption. When Ed baled Jonathan Gehman's hay, Joe exclaimed, *"da baler schaft!"* (The baler works!) Joe might have been skeptical before this, but now he was confident that Ed really had something.

When Ed offered Joe a partnership in the baler, Joe likely didn't want to be tied down. Ed was a thinker, Joe was a man of action. Joe didn't have the temperament for such a serious commitment. He preferred to fly by the seat of his pants. He learned easily in school and might have wondered if Ed's scheme would amount to much. Was he on a fool's errand? There were many other doubters in the neighborhood. Only later did he believe Ed really had something with this baler.

CAR SHOPPING

Ed was a man of few words. However, he also possessed the ability to use words to good advantage when the situation called for it. He listened with several other men as one in their group shared his dilemma regarding the purchase of a new car. In the past, Ed had helped the man through a particularly dire time of financial difficulties. Now recovered from his difficulties, he appeared to have forgotten them and, his boastful attitue was a bit too much for men.

He told them now he had visited a Lincoln showroom and wasn't sure if he liked what he saw, so he checked out the Cadillacs as well. Neither car completely satisfied his newly acquired, expensive taste and standards. "What do you think I should buy?" he asked Ed. Not wishing to nurture this man's hubris further, Ed replied, "I think if I were you, I would buy one of each!"

FURNITURE SHOPPING

A well-dressed Mennonite couple entered Good's Furniture Store just west of New Holland. The woman held a small dog. Richard Good, son of the store owner, met them and soon learned of their needs. They wanted a new dining room table, but none they saw seemed just right. The Good's home was quite close to the store, and Richard suggested they accompany him there to look at one more table. The table, quite expensive, was just what they wanted, and the young man wrote up an order. Later, conferring with his father, Richard said for some reason he didn't require of the couple the usual down payment needed to secure the order. Upon hearing a description of the couple, his father said he had made a wise decision. It was Ed Nolt and his wife.

AN UNUSUAL BALE TALE

Eddie remembers accompanying his father to work at New Holland in the old engineering building when he was 10 or 11 years old. One of his most enjoyable experiences was getting to drive the tractor while field testing. During a field test, Vera threw one of her brother Clarence's comic books in the windrow and it disappeared into the baler. Since the parents weren't very supportive of Clarence's reading materials, Vera didn't suffer any consequences from them. We don't know how Clarence reacted.

NO PICNIC

Vera remembers that the family never went to the New Holland employees' picnic, an annual event at New Holland Park. Ed said he was afraid people would ask him questions, and he wasn't one for small talk. Otto Luek brought the Nolts chicken corn soup and burgers grilled at the park.

A DUSTY HAT

Henry Fisher came to visit Ed at home during an illness. As they headed for a place to chat in another room, Henry took off his big, black hat and put it on top of the refrigerator. Observing this unexpected action, daughter Vera's immediate fear was one many women could share—what if the refrigerator top was dust! After she was sure the men had settled into their conversation, Vera retrieved Henry's hat from its high perch and made sure there was no offending dust on it. The visit came off without embarrassment and Vera's housekeeping reputation was still intact.

A REEL STORY

John Stahl-Wert and his grandfather Michael Wert, also father-in-law of the author, accompanied Ed on a Florida fishing trip one day. John remembers the impressive array of fish-finding and navigational technology on Ed's boat. When they arrived at their location fifty miles offshore, John watched with interest as Ed secured the fishing rods to the boat. He became even more curious when he saw the electric powered reels being attached to their gear.

He was soon hauling up groupers from the ocean's depths with the remarkable reel. As their catch numbers grew, John asked his grandpa who claimed the fish they were catching. The fish belonged to Ed because he was a captain without a commercial license, but once they were back at the dock, John could buy some fish. He didn't say if he bought any fish that day, but some forty years later, he still remembers the speedy craft and the technology Ed enjoyed so much.

Index

— B —

Bare, Elvin, 25
Bare, Harold, 25
Beam, Richard, 69, 112
Best, Al, 56
Brown, Joseph A., 67, 99, 111, 113, 114
Buchen, Curvin, 25
Buchen, Landis, 25, 71, 74
Buckwalter, Raymond D., 36, 37, 39
Burkholder, Charlie, 95
Burkholder, Doris, 97
Burkholder, Eugene, 95
Burkholder, Julia, viii, 88, 95, 96, 97, 98, 101, 113, 114, 116
Burkholder, Kenneth, vii, 70, 95, 111, 112, 114, 115, 116
Burkholder, Leon Ray, viii, 97, 108, 109, 110, 113, 116
Burkholder, Michael, 70
Burkholder, Richard, 95

— D —

Daffin, Irl A., 36, 37, 51
Dellinger, 37, 66
Delp, George C., vii, 36, 37, 39, 44, 49, 50, 52, 53, 56, 57, 61, 64, 70, 71, 72, 73, 74, 76, 77, 78, 79, 86, 97, 102, 109, 112, 114

— E —

Eberly, John H., 27, 32, 44, 62, 97
Ebersole, 74
Eby, Dick, 44
Eyster, Phil, 32, 35, 39, 40

— F —

Fisher, Henry, ix, 37, 42, 51, 66, 110, 124
Fisher, J. H., 77
Frankhouser, Brian, viii, 110, 114

— G —

Gehman, David, viii, 108, 116
Gehman, Jonathan, 11, 122
Glick, Ivan, 41, 66, 98, 99, 108, 109, 110, 111, 113, 114
Good, Aaron, 21, 23
Good, Merle, viii
Good, Phyllis Pellman, viii
Good, Richard, 123, 124

— H —

Halls, Larry, 44
Hertzler and Zook, 51, 66
Holiday, Jim, 58

INDEX

Hoober, Charles "Bud", 25
Hoover, Amos B., vii, 54, 111, 114, 116
Hoover, Henry, 24, 122
Horning, 56
Horning, Donald, vi, vii, ix, 110, 112, 115
Horning, Moses, Bishop, 55
Horning, Wilbur, 120
Hurst, Earl, 25
Hurst, Mabel Nolt, viii, 112, 113, 116
Hurst, Marlene, viii

— I —

Innes, Mr., 6

— K —

Kauffman, v
Kauffman, Clyde, 48
Knight, Willys, 21
Kurtz, Katie, 24, 79
Kurtz, Moses, 24, 28, 97

— L —

Landis, Ira D., 111, 115
Lapp, John A., Dr., 104
LaTourneau, Robert G., 76
Lindbergh, Charles, Jr., 75
Lindbergh, Charles A., 75
Luek, Otto, 58, 67, 124
Luttringer, Homer K., 92, 108, 109, 110, 115

— M —

Martin, Anna W., 7, 18
Martin, Henry, viii, 11, 40, 109, 116, 122
Martin, John, 24
Martin, Jonas, Bishop, 54, 55
Mast, A. D., 44
McDuffie, Jim, 58, 67
McGinnis, Howard, 32, 44

— N —

Nelson, Clarence J., 71, 72, 73, 78, 80, 111, 112, 115
Newswanger, R. Wesley, 108, 109, 115
Newton, Paul, 51
Nolt, Anna, 41, 74, 79, 93, 94
Nolt, Anna W. Martin, 7, 11, 18
Nolt, Annie, 73
Nolt, Clarence, 94, 124
Nolt, Ed, v, vi, vii, viii, ix, x, 1, 2, 3, 9, 14, 18, 19, 20, 24, 25, 26, 31, 34, 37, 38, 39, 44, 48, 51, 52, 53, 54, 56, 57, 58, 61, 62, 63, 65, 66, 67, 69, 70, 71, 72, 73, 74, 76, 77, 79, 92, 98, 99, 101, 102, 103, 104, 108, 109, 110, 111, 113, 114, 117, 118, 120, 124, 130
Nolt, Eddie, 93, 94, 124
Nolt, Edwin B., x, 3, 22, 27, 74, 87, 94, 100, 109, 112, 114, 115
Nolt, Edwin H., x, 3
Nolt, Ivan, 93
Nolt, Joe, 4, 7, 8, 10, 11, 17, 118, 119, 121, 122
Nolt, Katie, 97
Nolt, Mabel, 93
Nolt, Mary, 18, 93
Nolt, Mary Burkholder, x, 3, 7, 8

Nolt, Peter, 54
Nolt, Vera, 41, 93, 94, 124

— P —

Peters, Ed, 65
Peters, L. E., 111, 115

— R —

Rand, Remington, 65
Ressler, 122
Ressler, Bob, 65, 118, 120
Rubinson, 48
Ruth, William Chester, 23, 109, 115
Rutt, Galen, 111
Rutt, Mahlon, 111
Rutt, Phares, 86, 92

— S —

Sauder, 73
Sensenig, M. S., 93
Seymour, Howard, 58
Seymour, Mary, 56, 57, 59
Seymour, Shaun, vii, viii, 15, 18, 50, 53, 56, 57, 58, 59, 62, 88, 91, 102, 108, 109, 110, 111, 115, 116
Shirk, Allan W., v, vi, 104, 110, 111, 112, 114, 115, 130, 131
Shirk, Beverly, 131
Shirk, Jeff, 112
Shirk, Melissa, 131
Shirk, Ruth Ann, viii
Shirk, Ruth Ann Wert, 131
Sierk, Randy, 120

Skromme, Larry, 47, 56, 58, 62, 63, 64, 94, 95, 113, 115
Smoker, 66
Sperry, 65, 69
Sperry Rand, 66
Stahl-Wert, John, 125
Stauffer, Harry, 69
Steely, Bob, 62
Stone, Mr., 67
Sturla, Jim, 67
Sturla, Pete, 58

— T —

Tallman, Robert, 110, 115
Thiessen, Richard D., 111, 115

— W —

Wanner, Aaron M., 9
Weaver, Frank N., vii, viii, 8, 63, 88, 92, 94, 108, 109, 111, 112, 113, 115, 116
Weaver, Harvey, 8
Weaver, Lester, 25
Weaver, Luke, vii, viii, 79, 109, 116
Wenger, Joseph, 55
Wenger, Luke, 120, 121
Wert, Michael, 125
Wissler, Robert U., 112, 115
Wright, 48

— Y —

Young, Arthur S., viii, 4, 7, 23, 26, 27, 28, 31, 32, 34, 35, 40, 41, 42, 43, 44, 45, 106, 122
Young, Luetta, 28

— Z —

Zimmerman, Abe, 38, 39
Zimmerman, Ammon, 73
Zimmerman, George, 10, 13, 14, 25
Zimmerman, Raymond, vii, viii, 14, 15, 109, 116

The Author
MEA CULPA

I have found writing this book to be an interesting experience of listening to people's stories and memories of Ed Nolt. I am grateful for all who shared with me in this venture. While it has been my desire to tell this story as accurately as possible, I take responsibility for any errors of fact or judgement.

ALLAN W. SHIRK, BIOGRAPHY

Allan W. Shirk was born in East Earl, Pennsylvania, near New Holland. He remembers talking to neighbors and friends about their jobs at New Holland Machine Company. He also remembers hearing stories about Ed Nolt. As a boy, he enjoyed ice skating on Nolt's pond on the edge of New Holland, and wished he could go to the annual employee family picnic held at New Holland Park.

After earning his undergraduate degree at Eastern Mennonite College, Shirk received a M.Ed. in Social Studies Education at the Pennsylvania State University. In 1965 he began teaching social studies at Lancaster Mennonite High School. After 15 years of teaching at Western Mennonite School in Oregon, he returned to finish his career at Lancaster Mennonite School, retiring in 2010.

Mr. Shirk is married to Ruth Ann (Wert) Shirk. They have two grown children—Melissa and Beverly—and three grandchildren.